Introduction

This book began life as a series of handouts written to help adults on a course called Second Chance to Learn. Each year the handouts were altered and added to as each intake of students offered ideas and advice. It isn't complete yet. There's plenty of room for improvement, and as the Second Chance to Learn course changes, so will the Study Skills Handbook. Publishing it in its present form is a response to the numerous requests we have received for copies from individual students, and from course tutors all over the country.

The Handbook was written for a particular group of students — adults who had left school at minimum leaving age with few or no qualifications and who were returning to education many years later. It was written to help them to learn on a particular course — one which undertakes a study of history, politics and economics with the aim of enabling students to understand the decline of Merseyside and to take action to reverse it. That's why sections such as '*Preparing and Presenting a Case*', and '*Straight and Crooked Thinking*' are included, as well as the more usual topics such as essay writing and notetaking.

The Handbook was designed to be used as the basis for group work, not for individual study at home, though it has also been found useful by some students who have simply read it through alone and tried to follow its recommendations. It is not a workbook with exercises. Students who require a workbook for individual home study will find many excellent ones on the market. (See the bibliography on page 52 for details.)

A. HOW TO USE THIS BOOK: A NOTE TO STUDENTS

Most adults who decide to enrol on a course for the first time feel anxious. Few schools prepare their pupils to be able to study independently. Even students who have worked for G.C.E. 'O' level and 'A' level courses are often ill-equipped to undertake other courses. Those who spent their school days in the 'lower' streams copying from blackboards and books fare much worse. Whatever your own experience of school, you can learn successfully once you have acquired a few basic skills. This book will help you to do this.

If you have recently begun a course *talk to your fellow students about the difficulties you are encountering*. You will soon discover they are shared by most students. What can you do to overcome them? *Ask your teachers if a course of study skills can be arranged* which will help you to develop whatever skills you need for your chosen course of study.

If that's not possible, you could *get together with other students and work through this Handbook together*. You will need to decide which skills are most urgently needed. Set aside a couple of hours for each. Talk about the difficulties you are experiencing. Tell one another how you try to do them, give one another tips, show your work to members of the group. Read the relevant section in the Handbook and work out ways to do things. Then go off and try them. Or better still, if you have time, try them out in the group. You could easily try taking notes from a chapter or a book you have to read, and afterwards compare your different versions and explain them to each other. If you have to write an essay you could plan it together. When you go home to write it you will all produce your own individual essays. *This isn't cheating: it's co-operating*. If you decide to work together in this way, read through the section below '*A Note to Teachers*' for more ideas.

If you are not able to work together as a group (with or without a teacher), you can still find ways of getting better. Read through the relevant sections of the Handbook and try out the ideas in them. Then try reading some of the specialised workbooks listed in the reading list (bibliography) on page 52. Talk about any difficulties you are encountering with fellow students and with your teachers. Above all, be confident. Learning to study is no different from learning any other skill. With time and practice you will succeed. Think back over anything you've learnt to do already — driving a car, cooking, any skills you've needed at work — and remember how difficult it was at first, how confused you felt. But you succeeded eventually. You will again.

However you go about developing your study skills, remember that *this Handbook is not a rule book*. It contains *suggestions* about how to try out new skills. *Everyone learns in different ways* and you need to experiment and adapt until you find out what works best for you. If you begin by trying out the ideas in this book, you can move on to developing your own techniques.

Below you can read the introduction given to students on Second Chance to Learn when they are about to attend Study Skills Workshops as part of their course. It may help you to understand what we mean by study skills and what you will be able to do by the end of a study skills course.

Study Skills Workshops on Second Chance to Learn

"Lots of people go right through school without ever being taught how to study. For example we copy notes from the blackboard but don't learn how to take our own notes, or decide what it's important to write down as we are listening. Many of us leave school feeling very unsure about our ability to write. Some of us don't feel we can spell very well. Some of us can spell reasonably well, but don't feel confident about sorting out all our ideas and organising them to produce a persuasive essay. These are examples of what are called study skills — the skills everyone needs to learn and practise if studying something new is to become easy and pleasurable.

*Study Skills Workshops are designed to help you learn (or brush up) these skills. They are workshops, not lectures, and that means there'll be practical exercises to do each week to practise the skills and work to do at home to get more practice. We hope you'll be able to find time to do it, **because any skill can only be acquired by lots of practice.** When you want to learn to drive a car, you don't just read a book about it. You learn a bit of the theory first, then you go on the road and practise. And the longer you practise the better you get (hopefully!). Study skills are the same. You may learn about how to take notes early on, but it is only by practising this regularly, that you get to be able to do it easily and well.*

We hope too that the study skills you'll learn here will help you in other aspects of your life, and certainly if you go on to any further studying.

These are the aims of the Study Skills Workshops
By the end of the course you should

a) have the following knowledge:

1) Know how to study more effectively; how to use your time most efficiently; know your own strengths and weaknesses with regard to studying.
2) Know about a variety of techniques you might use to improve your notetaking, essay writing etc.
3) Know which textbooks and other aids are available to help you to improve your study skills.
4) Know about some of the various ways writers and speakers mislead the public.

b) be able to perform the following skills:

1) Organise a weekly study schedule (and stick to it!).
2) Write confidently — from short paragraphs to extended essays.
3) Take notes from books, speakers, T.V./ film (critically).
4) Join in and learn from group discussions; chair and be secretary in a group.
5) Compose an argument and deliver it orally in front of a group.
6) Use a variety of resources e.g. Library, Town Hall to find information.
7) Understand and read material presented as graphs and statistics.
8) Distinguish between 'straight' and 'crooked' thinking and argument, and be better able to detect when you are being misled (especially by the media).

c) develop the following attitudes:

1) Be confident about improving your learning, memory etc.
2) Enjoy learning: see difficulty as a challenge, a step towards learning, not as a problem.
3) Be co-operative, not competitive, about learning. Be willing to question your own and others' views about what is said and heard.''

LEARNING TOGETHER: A Study Skills Handbook
by Judith Edwards

CONTENTS

Preface

The ability to *study* is not something we are born with; neither is it a *gift* possessed by the chosen few. It is something we can all acquire and do well with practice, providing we are shown how. But we rarely are. Few schools actively teach their pupils how to study. Universities and colleges of higher education take it for granted that their students have acquired all the necessary skills before they arrive. How wrong they often are.

So many students either do less well than they could do, or even drop out of courses, because they cannot cope with the unfamiliar skills involved. This book arose directly from needs expressed by students who said, for example:

"You expect us to take notes and I've no idea where to begin."

"You suggest we read this newspaper or that chapter. I've never read a textbook in my life, just novels."

We decided to tackle this, not with individual students but *together in groups*. This collective approach worked. Students could learn from one another, as well as from a textbook and a teacher. They could share their ideas and, equally important, their anxieties about failing. This Handbook is the product of that shared learning experience. It is designed to be used in a series of Study Skills Workshops, but it has also helped students studying alone. It can be used by groups of students without the help of a teacher. Although it was devised for adult learners, it could be used equally well in schools, equipping school leavers to embark on further courses.

I would like to thank all the students I have worked with over the years. It's for them this book was written, and it's from them that many of the ideas and amendments have come. The Second Chance to Learn tutors have made useful contributions too. Special thanks go to Carol Byrne who not only typed the manuscript, but made helpful suggestions as she did so, making it more readily understandable.

Thanks go to the following, who have kindly given permission for the use of copyright material:
Scuola di Barbiana, Florence, Italy, for an extract from '*Letter to a Teacher*'
Liverpool City Planning Department, for graphs taken from '*Liverpool Planning Information Digest 1980*'.

Judith Edwards

B. HOW TO USE THIS BOOK: A NOTE TO TEACHERS

Every course requires different skills. If your course is based on group discussions, the skills needed (listening, contributing, presenting an argument etc.) will be different from those needed if you spend most of your time lecturing and answering questions. You will need to select relevant sections of this Handbook, and almost certainly the order of presentation will have to be altered. Some sections may be omitted. You may have to write additional sections yourself.

Most students benefit enormously from a separate course of Study Skills Workshops run alongside their main course. If plenty of time is available, several workshops could be devoted to practising each of the skills. If little time can be set aside for Study Skills Workshops, the practical element could be undertaken at home and the workshops used for sharing ideas and comparing experiences. But time and money may be so limited that this is impossible. If so, you could make time in your course to ensure students can acquire the skills they will need.

There are no set exercises in this Handbook. This is deliberate. It is impossible to set relevant tasks at a suitable level for a wide range of students on different courses. The book contains ideas. Each teacher must then supply suitable materials to work from. In this way the learning can be directly related to a particular course — allowing students to see how to adapt each skill to their own learning and to reap immediate rewards.

Some teachers have tried running Study Skills Workshops in advance of a course in order to prepare students. This rarely seems to work as well as workshops run alongside whatever courses students are engaged on. But if this is the only option available to you and your students, it will undoubtedly be better than leaving it to chance and hoping your students will 'pick up' the necessary skills.

Teaching study skills is of benefit to students. It is equally beneficial to tutors, because your students will be less confused and anxious, and as a result they will experience more success and be less likely to leave.

The description which follows of how the Handbook is used on Second Chance to Learn may serve as a useful guide which you can adapt.

Study Skills on Second Chance to Learn

Study Skills Workshops take place over 15 weeks. Each session lasts one hour and a quarter (though two-hour sessions would be much more valuable). Each student is issued with a copy of the Study Skills Handbook at the beginning of the course.

The following format is usually followed:

a) Students are asked to read the relevant section of the Handbook in advance.

b) For the first 15-20 minutes of each workshop students talk about the skills in question: their previous attempts at them; difficulties they have encountered; and solutions they have discovered. This part of the workshop is essential because *it helps the students realise that they are not alone in experiencing difficulties*, and that they can learn from one another, accepting suggestions from fellow students as well as from tutors and books. *It gives them confidence in their ability to acquire the skills.*

c) A few minutes are spent re-capping the Handbook section which was read prior to the session, and clarifying the ideas in it where necessary.

d) Then a task is tried by all members of the group. *The task is directly related to the content of the main course.* So, for example, when notetaking is practised, materials from the Second Chance to Learn course are used in the Study Skills Workshops. This is vitally important if the skills developed in workshops are to become part of each student's regular study routine.

e) After the task students compare their efforts — *not competitively*, but in order to see how others have approached the exercise. They talk about what they tried to do, what problems they encountered, and they are encouraged to offer tips to one another. The emphasis throughout is on *co-operation*: helping and learning from one another.

f) Finally the group discusses ways and opportunities of using the newly acquired skills regularly. Sometimes specific 'homework' may be set, but this should never be at the expense of helping students work out their own ways of using the skill. It is easy to fall into the trap of setting exercises with the result that, whilst students become competent at performing exercises, the skills do not become part of their day-to-day study.

One thing is certain: *everyone can learn to study*. A few students may pick it up as they go along just by returning to education. But most benefit greatly from a separate course of Study Skills Workshops closely integrated to the main body of the course they are studying.

As students on the Second Chance To Learn course have said:

"I'm no longer overwhelmed at the idea of written work or thinking about doing another course."

"I no longer have the fear of learning I had before."

"It makes the work easier knowing the right way to tackle it."

"It saves time and energy."

"I've come to realise that it's possible to learn how to study, that it isn't a God-sent gift."

If you require further information about the teaching of study skills, a chapter of a book on Second Chance to Learn is available from:
W.E.A. 7/8 Bluecoat Chambers, School Lane, Liverpool L1 3BX.
Please write for details.
A very useful book for teachers to read is:
Teaching Students to Learn: A Student-Centred Approach by G. Gibbs (Open University 1981).

Chapter 1

Solving Study Problems

In this chapter we shall look at the following:

● *some of the problems adults meet when they return to studying*

● *how to use the time you have effectively.*

All of us have problems when it comes to studying. Some of these are *outside* us, e.g. the baby, the telly, too much other work to do. Some of them are *inside* us, e.g. lack of confidence, finding it hard to get down to things.

All of us have advantages too, e.g. interest in a topic, determination.

To help you think about *your problems and your strengths* here are four profiles of imaginary students. Read through each profile and make three lists for each:

1) A list of the possible problems these students might face.

2) A list of possible solutions.

3) A list of the advantages they might possess which will help to overcome their problems.

After you have done this:

> ★ *Start thinking about your own problems and about how you can solve your problems* ★

Then make your own lists like this:

My Advantages
1. I'm really determined.
2. I can write well, despite spelling problems.
3. _____
etc.

My Problems
1. Too much housework etc. — not enough time.
2. I can't spell very well.
3. _____
etc.

Solutions
1. Husband/children do more housework.
2. Additional spelling classes?
3. _____
etc.

MAUREEN

Maureen is married and has four children between the ages of 7 and 15. Her husband has recently been made redundant and spends a lot of time at home, but is depressed and reluctant to help her with the housework. They have a small house, with no free rooms to study in. She has a part-time job in a pub four evenings a week which she can't really afford to give up.

She's very keen to learn, and longing to be able to understand all sorts of things she's never properly understood when she's heard about them in the news, or read about them in the papers. She'd like to be able to help her children with their schooling too. But she's very nervous about whether she'll be able to cope and she expects everyone else will be much cleverer than she is. She feels reluctant to open her mouth in case she makes a fool of herself, and she's worried about writing, especially essays.

She wants to be able to write better by the time she finishes the course, and she hopes to be more knowledgeable and confident, but beyond that she's not sure. In some ways she'd like to go on to study and get a better job. But she's worried about neglecting her family, and she's anxious about the money involved too.

Above all she just wants to have a really good go at this course, get out of it all she can, and then see what the future holds.

ADVANTAGES:

PROBLEMS: *SOLUTIONS:*

"Some of the problems adults meet when they return to studying."

KENNY

Kenny left school eight years ago and since then has never had any steady regular work. He used to be able to pick up casual work fairly easily, then after a few months he'd be back on the dole. For the last eighteen months he's been permanently unemployed and has few hopes of getting work.

At school he was bored and spent quite a bit of time truanting, and a lot of time messing around. He'd been keen and able at primary school but once he got into secondary school everything went downhill. Despite his lack of attendance he was bright enough to learn to write quite well (though his spelling's a bit shaky), and he could read anything he needed to.

Now he's decided he'll have to catch up on that lost schooling if he's ever going to get a decent job. He knows he's quite clever, but he feels as though he's forgotten everything he ever knew. But he doesn't like to admit it and is inclined to bluff if he thinks he might be caught out. He has mixed feelings about it all. On the one hand he's determined to make a go of it all, determined to take a first step towards some kind of new life. On the other he's not sure what he wants, and not even certain that this is the ideal course for him. It just seems a good starting point.

He'll have plenty of time to study, but he'll need to be very self-disciplined to use that time well.

ADVANTAGES:

PROBLEMS: *SOLUTIONS:*

DAVE

Dave works for a local firm and has managed to arrange to have a day a week off work — but unpaid — in order to come on this course. That's going to mean overtime, if he can get it, and less money for the family (his wife and three children). But, despite the hardship, he's determined to have a go.

He hates his job and only sticks it because it's reasonably well paid and there's little chance of anything else. He has been an active trades unionist for many years and has been on T.U.C. courses, but never on a general course of this kind. He's pretty confident he can manage it, though he's a bit worried about the money and about finding time to do any homework he may be set.

He's been doing some voluntary work (a Sunday Football Team) for years and has decided he'd really like to work with youngsters, perhaps as a probation officer. He hopes this course will lead him towards that. He wants to discover whether he'll be capable of going on to a full-time course to qualify for a new job.

He really enjoys a good discussion and can usually persuade people to see things his way, so he's looking forward to the discussions on the course. But he's a bit less keen about doing any writing. He'll try to find time to have a go, though. He's also looking forward to an 'easy day' off work each week and views it as a bit of a holiday.

ADVANTAGES:

PROBLEMS: *SOLUTIONS:*

JEAN

Jean has three young children: the eldest is eight and the baby is three. Her husband works as a long-distance lorry driver, so he's away quite a lot, but when he is home he gives her a hand. She has a few relations not too far away who can help by minding the children occasionally, but she doesn't like to put on them too often.

She's decided to come on a course mostly so that she can get out of the house, meet other people and talk about something interesting, not just about rising prices, household tips or local gossip. She likes her neighbours but feels bored with the sorts of conversations she has with them and has always felt a bit different. She went to a local toddler group and there a few mothers tried a short course. She really enjoyed it. So this course is really exciting her. She's not certain she'll understand it, or even enjoy it all, but a day of adult company and something new to talk about when her husband gets home are attracting her.

She doesn't know whether the childcare for her baby will work out or not, or what to do if any of the children are at home ill. Her mother is often ill too and Jean is expected to go round and help when she is, even though her other two sisters live nearby. These things worry her as she begins her new course. But she was good at school and enjoys writing (especially poems), so she wants to have a go.

ADVANTAGES:

PROBLEMS: *SOLUTIONS:*

★ *Now*
1)   Write down your own advantages and your problems, and begin to work out some solutions.
2)   Make a timetable of your week, like the one below. Write down all your commitments (work and leisure). See what time you have left for regular study and plan your own study timetable.

day	morning	afternoon	evening
Monday			
Tuesday			
Wednesday			
Thursday			
Friday			
Saturday			
Sunday			

3)   Try and read one or more of the study skills books listed below. They are helpful and reassuring.
*4)   Talk to your tutors, fellow students and family about your worries or difficulties. Together you **can** solve them.* ★

BOOKS FOR YOU TO READ

1)   *Studying* by T. Sullivan (National Extension College) whole book.
2)   *Learn How To Study* by D. Rowntree (MacDonald) Chapters 1 and 2.
3)   *How To Study Effectively* by C. Parsons (Arrow) Chapters 1 and 2.
4)   *Mastering Study Skills* by R. Freeman (Macmillan Master Series) Chapter 1.

Chapter 2

Memory and Studying

We all know that some people have better memories than others. We only have to watch T.V. programmes like 'Mastermind' to realise that. But most of us think our own memory is worse than other people's. There's a reason for this. When a group of us are together, if someone else remembers something that I've forgotten, then I feel my memory must be worse. But when I remember something, I assume that everyone else remembers it as well, so I don't think my memory is better.

*Whether our memories are good or bad isn't nearly so important as we think. The key is how **efficiently** we use our memories. A child using a lever and fulcrum can lift a weight that an adult couldn't manage. In the same way, good use of our memories, even if we think they are bad, will soon lead to improvement.*

"We all know that some people have better memories than others."

HOW TO IMPROVE OUR MEMORIES

So how can we learn to use our memories better? What steps can we take to improve them?

Some of these ideas may be obvious to you already. Some may be new.

1.   The first aid to memory is *interest*.
That's pretty obvious. All of us can think of things we've wanted to remember and things we've had no interest in (or even wanted to forget). It's *far* easier to remember what interests us. So it's important, as far as possible, to study subjects which interest us, or to find ways of developing an interest in subjects we need to study.

2. Another aid is *understanding*.

If we don't understand something we simply can't remember it. For lots of us that's where we go wrong. We try to absorb and remember things without first getting to understand them fully. We may remember for a short time, but never for long. So it's important to spend as long as is necessary in coming to understand something before we begin to attempt to remember it. In the long term, it saves time.

But even when we're interested and understand reasonably well, there are often lots of facts, dates, laws, rules, etc. which are really hard to memorise. *Don't despair!* There are lots of ways of making that drudgery of learning far easier and much more successful. Here are some tips which have been proved to work time and again, both by psychologists and by people trying to study.

3. *Little and often* is the golden rule.

If we have things we must commit to memory (whether it's something practical at work or at home, or whether we're preparing for an exam or test, like learning the Highway Code for a driving test), then we will remember far better if we spend a *short* time trying to memorise the facts, and repeat this *often,* rather than saving it all up for one long concentrated effort the night before.

How often do we need to repeat things?

Most forgetting takes place in the *first few hours* after we've learnt something. So it's important to revise a few hours after the first attempt, and a few hours again after that. The next day we may be able to remember if we revise the things once or twice. The following day it's easier still. After a short time, just glancing over it occasionally is enough. Obviously the longer and harder something is, the more frequent the repetitions need to be at first. To make this frequent revision easier, if we have something we really need to know, it's a good idea to put the points down on a postcard or in a notebook we can carry around and look at often throughout the day.

4. *Active* repetition is more useful than *Passive*.

What does that mean?

Passive repetition means re-reading something we wish to remember.

Active repetition means trying to *recall* things and then checking to see if we're correct. That works far better — it's amazing the difference it makes. There are several reasons why. Here are two of the most important:

a) To recall something we often have to put things into our own words and that makes it a part of ourselves. It's better to put things into our own words than try to remember the exact words we've read.

b) If we know we have to recall something we pay far more attention when we're reading, listening or watching something. That's the main reason our memories improve.

So if we are reading a book or listening to a speaker or watching T.V. we've got to keep stopping to *actively* recall. That's easy with a book or newspaper. We can stop every few pages (maybe every few lines if it's really hard), turn the book over and try to sum up what we've read. It may seem very time-consuming but it'll save a great deal of time in the end because we understand and remember better. Obviously it would be silly to do this with every book or paper we read. It's only necessary when we want to remember something.

It's harder to practise active recall when we're listening to somebody or watching T.V. since we can't stop them when we want to try to recall what's been said. Most people's answer to this is to make a few brief notes whilst listening, then to use these *immediately* afterwards to help us to recall. If what was said was really important to remember, then we need to use these notes, plus our fresh memories, to write it down. (See Chapter 6 for more information on note taking). Even doing this quite quickly and not very fully will improve our memories enormously.

Try it when you're watching T.V. news or current affairs programmes. Practise it regularly and find out for yourself how many notes you need to jog your memory. The most important part of this is doing the active recall stage as soon as possible after hearing what was said.

5. We remember best when we make use of what we've read and heard.

The easiest and probably the most useful way of making use of facts we've heard or read is having discussions with others about them frequently. That's quite a painless way to improve our memories (providing we don't bore our friends and family to death!).

Another way is to use the facts to prepare a case or an argument for or against something. That helps us to select facts, organise them, and then express the ideas for ourselves. Writing down our ideas is particularly useful.

Every one of these steps improves our ability to remember.

To sum up then:

- Passively reading and listening will achieve little: actively recalling is far better.
- Using the facts to do something else, like talking or writing about them, is better still.
- *At least* half of our study time should be active — not passive.

> ★ ***Do a mental check of all you've done this week and see whether you spent at least half your time actively. If you didn't — change your studying habits.*** ★

Doing all these things won't produce a brilliant memory overnight but it will improve your memory *a lot.*

BOOKS FOR YOU TO READ

1) *Learning to Study* by G. Gibbs (National Extension College) Chapter 4.
2) *How to Study Effectively* by R. Freeman (National Extension College) Chapter 2.
3) *How to Study Effectively* by C. Parsons (Arrow) Chapter 5.

Chapter 3

Learning from Discussion
Chairing a Group and Reporting Back

Lots of us enjoy discussions, but how much do we learn from them? This chapter looks at some of the problems that can hinder learning in group discussions and, in it, we will work out ways of having discussions which will allow everyone to learn. We'll also look at ways of getting better at chairing groups and reporting back.

> ★ *Think about some discussions you've been involved in, or watched on T.V. or in meetings. Think about a good discussion, one which worked well and helped you to learn. Write a list of the things that happened which made that discussion successful. How did people behave? How did they put over their ideas? Why did you enjoy it? Then think about a discussion which didn't work well, and write a list of the things which spoiled it. Compare your lists with those of your fellow students, and try to work out for yourselves some useful rules for discussion groups. Then compare your list with the one below which Second Chance To Learn students have produced.* ★

A.   SOME GROUND RULES FOR DISCUSSION

Learning from discussion involves:

- pooling ideas
- being ready to listen to students and tutors and to learn from them
- being willing to explore our ideas with others and accepting that we may need to alter them in view of what we hear from others
- being non-competitive, not trying to out-do others.

To make all of this work it's important to agree some 'ground rules' to make discussion groups work well. Here are some suggestions. Perhaps you have others.

> ★ *In your group, work out a set of ground rules you can all feel happy with.*
> *Try them out for a while, then set aside some time to talk about how well*
> *they are working. Make changes in your ground rules if you need to.* ★

1)   Before the discussion session write down your questions or opinions so you have them with you. That way you won't be over anxious to say your bit in case you forget it. It will also ensure that there are plenty of ideas to discuss.

2)   During the discussion, when you get an idea of your own or have a comment to make on someone else's, jot it down so you won't forget it. This too will ensure that there are plenty of ideas to discuss.

3)   When someone has suggested an idea or opinion, follow it through. If you were about to express an unrelated idea, save it and think about the idea that's just been expressed and comment on that idea if you wish. Avoid making a series of unrelated comments.

4)   Listen carefully to each speaker and don't interrupt. Think about what she or he has said. What other students say is just as important as what the tutor says.

5)   Try to make sure everyone has a chance to speak if they wish. If you're shy, make an effort to speak up. Everyone will listen. If you know you talk a lot, look around and ask others their opinion. Don't wait for the tutor to do this, and don't jump in every time there's a silence: let someone else break it.

6) If you think the discussion has strayed away from the point, say so. Don't wait for the tutor to do this all the time.

7) Don't talk for too long. Make your point simply and clearly, so others will get a chance to say what they think.

8) If you're not certain you understand what's been said by a student or the tutor, *ask*. If *you* don't understand, probably most of the group don't either, but everyone feels embarrassed to ask.

9) If everyone seems to have similar opinions it's rather hard to learn anything new, so don't be afraid to suggest other opinions (even if you personally don't hold them) so they can be aired and discussed.

10) If someone seems to have different opinions from yours, don't shoot them down. Ask questions to try to understand their views and then work out how you disagree. Everyone's views are worth hearing.

Talk about these suggested ground rules with your group. Change them. Add to them. When you've finally agreed your own rules, try to stick to them for a while to see how they work, then review them and alter them again if necessary. Don't be afraid to talk about how your group works together. You have to do this if you are going to work well and learn from one another. Sometimes there are difficulties about how people get on together in groups, which hinder everyone's enjoyment and learning. It's best to discuss these openly but sensitively. This is all part of learning how to learn together.

"Sometimes there are difficulties about how people get on together in groups."

B. CHAIRING A GROUP AND REPORTING BACK

In many courses the main group may divide into smaller workgroups and each of these is asked to discuss particular questions. Sometimes they are asked to read materials to help them. After the small group discussion each workgroup reports back its conclusions to everyone in the main group. The conclusions of each workgroup are then compared and discussed together.

To carry out these tasks each workgroup needs a *Chairperson* and a *Reporter*.

During your course you may be encouraged to take a turn at chairing workgroups, and also at reporting back from your workgroup. These are very useful skills to develop, particularly if you become involved in groups outside your course. People are often very reluctant to take on these important jobs. If you try them out on your course you will hopefully feel confident enough to take them on in other groups.

C. WHAT JOBS DOES A CHAIRPERSON HAVE TO DO?

1. Deciding what needs to be discussed, and in what order things should be discussed.
Sometimes this involves planning the agenda in advance of a workgroup or a meeting. It may involve looking carefully at the tasks your group has been set, deciding in what order to tackle them, how much time to allow for each, and distributing reading materials to ensure that each piece is read by at least one group member.

2. Ensuring a balanced contribution from different group members.
If some people are shy and reluctant to say much, it means helping them to do so, but doing this sensitively so that shy people don't feel they've been put on the spot. If others are very ready to talk, it may be necessary to encourage them to listen more, asking them to hold back for a while until others have had a turn. Again this requires tact. If someone is straying off the point, perhaps telling a long story to illustrate some point, you may have to stop them by pointing out that you don't have enough time to go into all of that, however interesting it may be.

It isn't your job to get everyone to agree. Differences of opinion are important and a necessary part of any discussion. You haven't failed if you can't get everyone to agree. Quite the contrary. So you need to help those with differing views to air their differences clearly so that they, and everyone else, can understand them.

Generally a Chairperson has to *control the discussion but not dominate it*. A Chairperson is more likely to ask questions than give opinions.

3. Ensuring that everyone understands all that has been said.
You can do this by asking the group from time to time whether they have understood points or whether they wish to ask any questions. You may need to ask questions yourself, if you don't understand something, or if you think others don't.

4. Ensuring that the person who is to report back is getting the relevant information down.
This means you have to stop once an answer has been given, check whether the group generally feel that it is an important point, and then ask the reporter to note it down and read it back to the group. If you do this job well, everyone will be clear about the discussion, and the reporter's job will be a much easier one.

It's also helpful from time to time to ask your reporter "Where have we got to now?" A brief report back will help everyone feel clearer about the discussion and will help it to move forward.

5. Keeping an eye on the time.
Make sure you are sticking to your timetable so that every question can be answered.

6. Reserving five minutes at the end to let your reporter read back her/his report.
This helps you all to feel clearer about what you've discussed. It also lets you check whether the reporter has everything down clearly. And it gives the reporter the chance to try out the report on you, before taking it back to the main group.

D. WHAT DOES A REPORTER HAVE TO DO?

1) Taking notes.
a) In order to report back you need to take notes of important points. *The problem is deciding which points to take note of*. Your Chairperson will be helping you to decide this by regularly stopping the discussion and summing up the main points for you.

b) If you're not sure which points to put down, *don't be afraid to ask for help*. It's easy to ask the group "Do you want me to report this back?" and if they do, make a note and read it back to them to check it's correct. If you do this it's very helpful to everyone else in the group, because you can't make notes unless you fully understand what's been said; and if you haven't understood it, you can be fairly certain other members of your group didn't understand either, so your questions will help them too.

c) *Don't take too many notes*. You aren't trying to reproduce the full discussion point by point, comment by comment. You're just noting the points you all agree are important.

d) There will be times when not everyone will agree. There will be important minority opinions. If so, check whether the group wants the minority opinions reported back, and if they do, make a note of them too.

e) *Read your report back to your group* at the end to check that you've got it right. You may need to alter it a bit at this stage to make it clearer to those who weren't in your group.

2) Giving the report back.
Because most people are nervous they often just read a list of points, offering no explanation, and quickly sit down again. Report backs done like this tend to leave others confused. It's easy to do a much clearer report back.

a) If possible *write up the main points* on a large sheet of paper so that everyone can see it as you speak.

b) Then *explain briefly but clearly what each point means*. Go through the points one by one and if any of your listeners don't understand a point let them ask questions. Either you, or any other member of your group, can explain it.

c) *Avoid reading the notes*. Use them to prompt your memory and then *talk*. Just explain it, as you all explained your ideas in the workgroup.

d) *Above all don't worry about it*. If you haven't made something clear, you, or someone else, can explain again. Nothing is lost. You will get better and better at this as your confidence grows.

With regular practice of chairing and reporting you should in time feel confident enough to undertake these jobs whenever the need arises.

Chapter 4

Reading to Learn

Reading a textbook, or even just a part of it, can be a real headache, and some of us can never get round to it. This chapter will help you in the followings ways:

- *finding your way around a textbook and choosing what to read*

- *learning to skim rapidly through a book or chapter*

- *learning to be critical and questioning, but not resistant*

- *improving your reading speed.*

A. INTRODUCTION

Everyone reading this book can read, but many of us say we want to *improve* our reading. What do we mean by this?

★ ***Stop and think what you mean by this. Write down your ideas.*** ★

You may have thought of some of the following points:

- we want to read *faster*

- we want to be able to *understand* better what we're reading

- we want to be able to *remember* what we've read.

These points, and some others, will be discussed in this chapter. But before we begin to look at them, let us take a broader look at reading first.

Most of us read in the same way we used to at the age of ten. Few secondary schools pay any attention to developing reading skills (except for those children who have special difficulties). Many of us think of ourselves as 'poor readers', and in some ways we may be. Perhaps we never vary our reading speed according to the difficulty or importance of the material; or we don't concentrate or read purposefully, and so forget most of what we read.

There are several ways of reading, each appropriate for different purposes:

1. Scanning.
This is very rapid reading where we are searching for a particular piece of information — a date or name perhaps — and totally ignore the rest of the text. We do this, for example, when we look in the car sales column of the local newspaper.

2. Skimming.
It's rather similar to scanning. It involves looking very quickly at everything, but *not* searching for anything in particular. It's useful when we want to get an overall impression of what the book/article/chapter is about before reading it carefully. Skimming is a very important first stage of reading a textbook, but many of us don't bother to do it, we just plunge straight into the 'heavy' reading.

3. Light reading.
Reading newspapers/novels etc. for pleasure. If you now read these slowly and laboriously, this is where you can start practising speeding up — using the tips you'll find later on in this section under the heading '*Faster Reading.*'

4. Reading to learn.
The remainder of this chapter is concerned with reading to learn and looks at how we can improve our ability to do this.

B. READING TO LEARN

When we are reading to study and learn, whether as part of a course or simply to understand something we are interested in, the first point to remember is that it's important to be *critical and questioning, but not resistant*.

This means that at all times we should be questioning what we are reading, asking questions like this:

"What is this about — what's the main idea?"

"Why should I believe this — where's the proof?"

"Is this a fact or an opinion?"

"Do the conclusions follow from the facts?"

"Do I agree with the conclusions?"

etc.

Doing this is being questioning and critical, but it's easy to slip into being negative or resistant. If we don't much like the author's ideas we refuse to really try to understand and only seek to disprove them. A questioning and critical attitude is positive. It arises out of a desire to get at the truth. Resistance is negative.

Keeping in mind the need to be critical and questioning, but not resistant, how do we go about improving our ability to read effectively and get the most out of the time we spend reading, whether it's a little or a lot?

Many people recommend the following 5 stages when reading for understanding, which are often referred to as SQ3R. They are:

1. **S**urvey

2. **Q**uestion

3. **R**ead

4. **R**ecall

5. **R**eview

Notice that only one of the 5 stages is the actual reading. You may think that this is going to be a very inefficient way of spending what time you can spare for reading, since it's clearly going to take longer than simply picking up a book and reading it. Well, it will take a bit longer *initially*, but it will also *save a great deal of time in the end*. For example, in the *survey* stage you may well decide not to read the book at all, or only to read a short relevant passage, and that will save the time it would have taken to read an irrelevant book. Following these five stages will also ensure that you understand the book a lot better and remember it better too. In other words *you will improve your reading*.

Let us look at each of these 5 stages in turn to see just what's involved.

1. Survey.
This means *looking over a book to find out what's in it without actually reading it*.

a) Look for the following information:
   Title
   Author
   Date of first publication and date of this edition.

b) Read the Preface, the Introduction and the 'blurb' if there is one. (The dustcover of a hardbacked book, or back cover of a paperback, has a 'blurb' — a short description of the book.)

c) Look at the contents page.

d) Look at the index.

Doing this will often give you enough information to decide whether this book is going to be useful to you. But the survey can go a lot further than that.

e) Look at each chapter in turn. If it has subheadings or a summary at the end, read these.

f) To get an idea of what the chapter is about, try reading the first and last paragraphs.

g) If you want more information before beginning to read, skim through the chapter very rapidly. This can involve reading the first and last sentences of each paragraph quickly and glancing over what lies between them. *Try this skimming and you'll be surprised at how much information you can glean very rapidly*. You'll also discover how much easier it is to read a difficult text when you've already surveyed and skimmed it, have a sense of direction and know what's coming next.

2. Question.

If you are to be a critical and questioning reader *it's very important to think about what questions you want answered before you begin to read*. If you do this, you'll read purposefully, you'll understand a great deal better and, because your attention is concentrated, you'll remember what you've read. It will also be a lot easier to make notes because you know what you're looking for. Some useful general questions are written on page 19. You can add to these some more specific questions on the particular subject you are reading about. The headings and subheadings will often suggest new questions to you.

Above all you should always be asking yourself "*What's the main point that's being made*?" Every book has a main point; every chapter in it has a main point; and every section of a chapter has a main point. Only when you can understand the main points will you be able to understand the book properly. You also need to find the main points in order to be able to write notes.

"Every book has a main point … Only when you can understand the main points will you be able to understand the book properly."

3. Read.

Only now are you ready to read. Instead of reading laboriously word by word, as most of us do when something is hard, try reading it through very quickly twice. You'll probably discover that you understand it a lot better that way. If it's really hard to understand, you may want to have one quick read, followed by a slower one. But the first reading should always be a quick one. Then as you read for the second time, remember to be looking for answers to the questions you thought of, and thinking of some new questions too. You may need to read it through more than twice.

Do so if it's necessary. It isn't a waste of time if it leads to understanding. When you first rapidly read a chapter you're simply trying to grasp what the author is saying. *Only when you fully understand the author's case can you begin to criticise it*. If you criticise too soon you'll fail to listen to the author and may be carried away by your own ideas, so there will have been little point in reading the chapter.

4. Recall.
You may want to start to recall after you have read the whole chapter or, if the chapter is quite long or complicated, it may be necessary to recall after each section. Recalling means trying to *remember* all the main ideas in the section or chapter and preferably *writing them down*. This is the stage to make notes — not whilst you are reading. If you look back to Chapter 2 on '*Memory*', you will see that actively recalling what you've read is the most important part of improving your memory. Recalling will often take as long as, and sometimes longer than, the reading stage.

5. Review.
This simply involves looking back over what you've read then checking whether your recall was correct. Don't forget this stage, or you may be recalling things which are incorrect. Remember the questions you wanted to ask. Can you answer them now? Do you have any more questions? Tidy up your notes at this stage, adding any important information or ideas you'd forgotten.

C. FASTER READING

Most of us would like to be able to read faster than we can; and most of us, in fact, could double our reading speed with a few weeks of practice. But *the important thing is to **understand** what we read, not to get through it as fast as possible*. Some material can't be read quickly and reading it slowly isn't a sign of failure.

But some things can and should be read quickly — light novels, newspapers, magazines etc. You can practise reading these quickly. Gradually you'll be able to read harder material more quickly too.

Let us first look at the *causes of slow reading* and how to remedy some of them.

1. Poor eyesight (constant blurring).
Remedy — Go to an optician to have your eyesight checked.

2. Unfamiliarity with the subject.
If a subject is new to you and has a lot of unfamiliar vocabulary and ideas, you are *bound* to read slowly. *Remedy* — Doing a lot of reading about a subject will help a lot. Mastering the unfamiliar words is important. Build up your own *personal dictionary* by keeping a notebook and writing down all the unfamiliar words. Find out what they mean. Use the new words in speech and writing until they become completely familiar.

3. Narrow vocabulary.
This is very similar to the above problem. *Remedy* — It too can be remedied by reading widely, looking up and writing down the meanings of unfamiliar words.

4. Saying every word under your breath when you read.
This means you read as slowly when reading silently as you would when reading aloud. *This is a very common problem*. There's no easy answer. But forcing yourself to read faster — preventing yourself saying every word — gets easier and easier to do with practice. *Remedy* — Try to sweep your eyes very quickly across each line. You'll discover you *can* take it in. Very fast readers often read down the page instead of zigzagging across every line. Try pointing your finger in the middle of the page and drawing it straight down, forcing your eyes to follow it, instead of reading every line carefully. You'll get a lot of understanding without looking at every word. Try this on light reading. Newspaper columns are good for practising on because every line is short anyway.

5. Reading every word separately and going back over words or groups of words for a second look.
Again this is a very common problem. *Remedy* — It can be dealt with by forcing yourself to keep going, forbidding yourself to go back. You can do this if you practise. You'll discover you actually understand the material better, because going back over things and reading the material slowly word by word can mean you forget the whole sentence or passage whilst you are slowly poring over one part of it.

Many people find that if they practise doing these things for just a short period, perhaps 15-20 minutes per day, they can improve the speed of their reading immensely.

But don't forget that *you can't read everything fast*. You must learn to *vary* your reading speed according to the material. Once you are good at reading faster, the skimming or rapid first reading needed before you read something will become much easier. Don't forget that once you've read something rapidly you need to stop and *think* about what you've read and try to answer the questions you've been asking. *Rapid reading doesn't mean rushing through without thought.*

BOOKS FOR YOU TO READ

These are some useful books which explain about reading in much greater depth and provide a number of passages and timed exercises to help you work at improving your reading speed if you want to:

1) *Read Better: Read Faster* by M. and E. De Leeuw (Penguin).
2) *Speed Reading* by T. Buzan (David and Charles)
3) *Reading and Understanding* by T. Sullivan (National Extension College) Chapter 2.
4) *How to Study Effectively* by R. Freeman (National Extension College) Lesson 3.
5) *Learn How to Study* by D. Rowntree (Macdonald) Chapter 5.
6) *Mastering Study Skills* by R. Freeman (Macmillan Master Series) Chapter 3.
7) *How to Study Effectively* by C. Parsons (Arrow) Chapter 3.

Chapter 5

Notetaking from books

When you are reading and studying, do you find it hard to work out what notes you need to make and how to organise them so that you can understand them weeks or months later? This chapter should help, with practical ideas to try. Taking notes helps us all to study more successfully and, equally important, allows us to collect information that we may need when we want to build up a case to convince others.

A.   WHY TAKE NOTES?

1.   To help understanding.
You don't retain much of what you read unless you stop frequently and recap — that is sum up what you've read in your own words. You should do this at least at the end of every chapter, or after every section of a long chapter. If it's hard to understand, you may need to do it after every paragraph. Imagine you're trying to explain the main point to someone else in your own words. Say it to yourself first, then write down what you've said.

2.   For interest.
Your interest usually increases the more you actively try to understand what you've read.

3.   For re-use.
Notes can be used:

a) to help you write essays.

b) to prepare for exams — if you have to take them.

c) most important of all, to look back over regularly when you need to refresh your memory of facts and ideas, and improve your understanding, either for yourself or to help you make an explanation to others.

4.   To help you evaluate and criticise the author's ideas.
By trying to sum up an argument, you can often see when it doesn't follow logically.

What you need

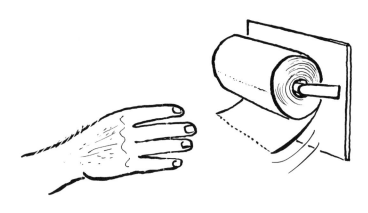

"You can use: a) scraps of paper." (See page 24).

B. WHAT YOU NEED

1. You can use:

a) scraps of paper

b) an exercise book or

c) best of all a *loose leaf ring folder*.

By using this you can group together notes from different books, lectures etc. under subject headings. You can add to (and take away from) your notes as you learn more about a subject.

2. Different coloured pens
These are a great help.

C. ABBREVIATIONS

You can work out a system of abbreviations yourself, provided you'll remember it later, and provided, if your notes will be read by others, they'll understand too. Once you've worked out a system, *stick to it*. It's a good idea to keep a 'key' to your abbreviations until you get used to them. Or you could put up a list somewhere where you can see it clearly and add to it as you discover new abbreviations. A shared list in the college (or wherever you learn) is a good idea.

Here are some of the commonly used abbreviations:

e.g.	for example		i.e.	that is
&	and		N.B.	note well/ this is important
>	greater than		<	less than
=	equals/ is the same as		≠	does not equal/is different
∴	therefore		∵	because

There are many commonly used ways of shortening words too, e.g. by missing out the middle letters. Here are a few:

c'd	could		w'd	would
Govt.	Government		educ^n	education

You could easily work some out for yourself and soon get accustomed to using them.

D. HOW TO MAKE NOTES

Before you even begin to read a book, and certainly before you begin to make written notes, *you must survey the book first*. Chapter 4, pages 19 and 20, explains 'surveying' in much more detail. Once you have carried out your survey you'll have an idea of what the book or chapter is about and what you're hoping to get from it.

1. First of all always note the title, author, publisher and date of a book, or the name and date of a newspaper article etc., so if you want to return to it later you can.

2. Leave lots of space between your notes so you can add and change things later if necessary.

3.
a) Generally it's best to read the chapter quickly through and get main ideas.

b) Make a note of what the chapter as a whole is about, in one or two sentences only.

c) Then re-read carefully and begin to make notes. Try doing it this way:

Read a section or paragraph through. Put the book aside and try to sum up the main points briefly, clearly and *in your own words. Don't* copy chunks from the text. Only when you've had to put it into your own words will you have fully understood it. If the section has a heading it can help if you use the heading too and expand on what it's saying.

d) Work through each section like this.

e) When you've completed the process, again try to sum up the main theme of the chapter in a couple of sentences. Check back on what you wrote at the beginning (3b) and see if you still want to say that or if you now feel you need to change it.

f) When you have finished look back over your notes and see that they are logical and make sense to you now. If they don't, re-read whichever parts are giving trouble. If your notes don't make sense to you *now* they certainly won't later!

E. WAYS OF WRITING NOTES

There are several ways of laying out your notes. It's best to try all of them and see which you feel happiest with and which are more use to you later when you want to re-use them. It's worth persevering in learning how to make notes in a variety of ways.

1.   Writing on the book.
The easiest way is to *make notes on the book or paper* (if it's yours to keep), underlining key words or phrases, ticking if you strongly agree, crossing when you don't and putting a question mark when you are unsure of the meaning. You can also jot comments in the margins.

It's quick and easy but *the least useful method* because you don't have to make any effort to understand and put it in your own words, so you may not even notice that you haven't grasped the main theme. If you do use this method, it should really only be *as a first step* towards making your own notes later. Another disadvantage is it's very hard to re-use notes like these, and you'll end up having to re-read the whole book or chapter later on.

2.   Summary notes.
You write about what you've read *in your own words*, as a piece of continuous prose, in complete sentences. So it's really just a shortened version of the original. (This is sometimes called a 'précis'.)

How to make summary notes
a) After you've read the whole article, chapter or whatever, write a short paragraph stating briefly what the whole thing is about.

b) Then go back to the beginning and work on each paragraph separately. Read it through and write it *briefly* in your own words, adding whatever details you feel are essential. To avoid copying the author's words, it's best not to look at the paragraph until you've finished your own summary.

c) Perhaps several paragraphs all refer to the same idea. If so, you can put them together in one paragraph of your own.

d) Some paragraphs may not say anything you feel is particularly important. If so, you don't need to write anything.

e) When you've finished going through like this, you may find it helpful to write a short concluding paragraph, summing up the whole article. This will probably be similar to your first paragraph. If it's more or less the same, don't bother.

Advantages.
As well as providing you with the notes you need, this method helps to develop your writing ability and style.

Disadvantages.
i)   It takes longer to do it this way — and you may lose the main points whilst you're worrying about how best to write things down.

ii)   Without headings etc. it's hard to see at a glance what it's about, so these notes are harder to revise from or reuse.

iii) It's hard to 'picture these notes in your head' afterwards and so harder to remember them.

3.   Outline.
This is the most popular way of making notes. You use key words and phrases — not full sentences — and you use headings and subheadings. Usually outline notes are arranged in a numbered sequence.

> ★ *Look back over these notes which you've just been reading. They are basically outline notes though I've used full sentences because they're not just for my own use. Check my headings and numberings. The main themes are lettered A B C D etc. In each section the subheadings are numbered 1, 2, 3 and in each of these there are letters a) b) c) etc. to further subdivide.* ★

How to make outline notes.

a) If the author has used a title or heading, either use that or else express the main idea of the article, chapter etc. briefly in your own words as a title.

b) For each section or paragraph work out what is the main idea or theme and use that as a subheading, summing it up in just a few words (maybe just one word).

c) Under each of those headings note down any *important* details or explanations. If any example has been given which helps you to remember, you can add that too, perhaps in brackets.

   Lay out these details or explanations separately with each new idea on a fresh line and leave plenty of space.

d) Look back over your notes and see whether *a system of lettering or numbering will make it clear which ideas belong together*. Many people just list items from 1 to 10 or 20 or whatever, but although that's reasonably helpful it doesn't make things as clear as deciding to use letters and numbers (in the way they've been used in these notes for example).

e) If possible use different *colours* to separate items, and use diagrams, drawings etc. where helpful to make the outline more memorable.

Advantages.

i) The main advantage of outline notes is that *you have to think hard* to do them. You have to work out the headings, and which details belong under which heading. All this greatly contributes to your understanding of what you've read, and this in turn will help you remember.

ii) They're also easier to glance through, easier to picture in your mind and easier to follow than summary notes.

Disadvantages.

i) The main disadvantage is that at first they are harder to write than a summary and may take you longer until you get the hang of it.

Remember — any way of making the notes memorable is a help — so that you can close your eyes and bring the notes back to mind as a picture. Try this one for example:

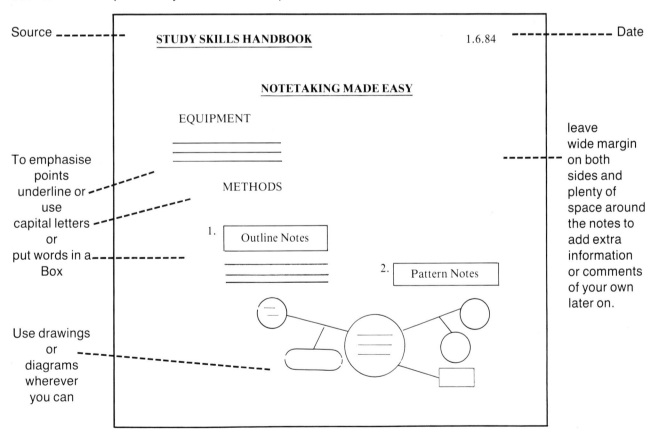

With a page of notes like this you should be able to close your eyes and bring the notes back to mind.

> ★ *Try it now with the example above. Look at it carefully, then close your eyes and see how much you can remember. Then open any other book, read a page of print, close your eyes and try to picture what it says. Which is easier to remember?* ★

4. Pattern notes.

Not many people use these, but those who master the knack often say they are much the most useful, so give the method a few tries and see if it will help you.

How to make pattern notes.

a) You begin by stating the topic in the middle of your page (see the example below). You can lay the page on its side — it's often more convenient.

b) In these notes only use single words or short phrases.

c) Link each main idea to the central point by drawing a line, then try to state what the main idea is in one or a few words and underline it.

d) If you want to add details for each main idea put them below the underlined heading (as in the example below). Or you can draw a box or circle around both the heading and the details to show they all belong together.

e) You can, if you wish, arrange these themes or ideas by putting the most important ones nearer to the central heading, the less important ones further away (this has not been done in the example below). If two or more themes or ideas seem particularly closely related, you can put arrows or lines between to emphasise the link.

f) Some students find that if they are making notes on a whole book or a long article these can't all be fitted on one sheet of pattern notes. So first they make outline or summary notes, then at the end they sum up all the *main points* of the book or article onto one sheet of pattern notes and place this at the front of their set of notes. In this way they can see at a glance all the main ideas and how they relate to each other, whilst the following sheets of notes supply the necessary detail.

Below is an example of pattern notes

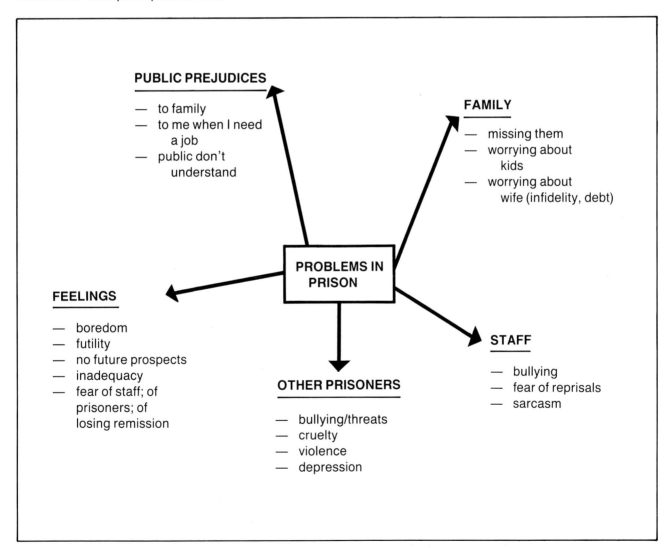

This method can also be used when you are *making notes for an essay*. (See Chapter 7.)

Advantages.

i)   These notes are quicker to write, and to read afterwards because they use only single words or phrases. They save paper too.

ii) Because the finished product is in the form of a diagram, it's usually much easier to remember and picture in your mind afterwards.

iii) Because the notes resemble a diagram and because all the ideas are represented on one page, it's easier to see the relationship between ideas, which are more important and how they all link up.

iv) Because there is space around each theme or idea, you can add any additional information later in the most appropriate place, instead of having to tack extra notes on to the end, as you would with summary notes.

v)   Most important, to produce a set of pattern notes you have to think hard, not just about what you've read, but about how the ideas relate to each other, and this naturally improves understanding and memory.

Disadvantages.

i)   As with outline notes, the main disadvantage is that until you get used to producing pattern notes it can take a lot longer. But it's well worth practising until they become easy to do.

(For more practice see Tony Buzan's book "Use Your Head.")

F.   CONCLUSION

However you decide to lay out your notes — summary, outline or pattern — it's important to *re-group and organise them later* as you learn more about the subject. If you've left plenty of space between the different parts of your notes you'll be able *to add your own ideas and comments*, or any new piece of information you may acquire later on. It's a good idea to use a different coloured pen for your comments and opinions, so that when you come to read the notes later you can easily tell which ideas were the author's and which were your own.

Once you have written the notes they'll have served their main purpose, because the concentration and mental effort required to make good notes will mean that you will have understood the subject far more deeply, and are likely to have put it into some order in your own head which will ensure that you'll remember it. Even if you lost your notes soon afterwards you'd still have benefited. Good notes mean that you can very quickly remind yourself about a topic, and used regularly they can ensure that you don't forget the subjects over a longer period of time.

BOOKS FOR YOU TO READ

1) *Learn How To Study* by D. Rowntree (Macdonald) Chapter 7.
2) *How To Study Effectively* by C. Parsons (Arrow) Chapter 4.
3) *Use Your Head* by T. Buzan (BBC Publications).
4) *Reading and Understanding* by T. Sullivan (National Extension College) Chapter 1.

Chapter 6

Notetaking in Lectures and Meetings

Most of us find it much harder to take notes when we are listening to a speaker or a lecturer, or when we are in a meeting or discussion, than to take notes from books. Do you listen to someone in a meeting or on T.V. and find afterwards that you can't really remember what was said? When you try to take notes, do you find you miss half of what they are saying whilst you are writing things down? When you look at your notes a few days or weeks later are they meaningless? This chapter offers suggestions for overcoming these problems.

A.   WHY IS IT SO DIFFICULT?

Few people seem to find notetaking whilst they are listening easy. That's one reason why most of us are so reluctant to volunteer as secretary to a group. Many adults who drop out of courses say they couldn't keep up with the lectures. Often they mean they couldn't take notes.

1.   It's faster.

It's harder to take notes from a lecturer or in meetings than from a book because *it's all so much faster*. We have to listen, analyse, select the important points and then write them down, whilst continuing to listen and think about the next point the speaker is making. We can't ask the speaker to keep stopping whilst we write our notes, or to keep repeating a point. But there is *one* major advantage worth remembering. If there's something we don't understand we can ask the speaker to explain it more fully. (We can't do that with a textbook!)

2.   The importance of practice.

So how can you develop this undeniably complicated skill? With practice. It really does become much easier. It's rather like learning to drive. At first you can't believe you'll *ever* be able to remember where each gear is, use the accelerator, clutch and brakes, as well as the lights and signals, whilst concentrating on keeping the car moving in a straight line *and* watching out for the other traffic! Yet in time it all becomes second nature. Have confidence that taking notes will too.

3.   Work out your own method.

There are some useful guidelines to help you listed below.

> ★ *Try them out, ask other people what they do, and work out a method that
> suits you best.* ★

Remember too that if you are regularly practising taking notes from books, then this will undoubtedly improve your skill and confidence in taking notes in lectures and meetings.

> ★ *Before reading on, look back at Chapter 5 'Notetaking from Books' to remind
> yourself about abbreviations and about different ways of laying out your
> notes when you come to write them up after the lecture or the meeting.* ★

B.   WHAT TO DO

1.   Preparing yourself.

If you know what the lecture or discussion is going to be about, try to *read up about it beforehand*. That way you'll get far more out of it, and it will be easier both to understand and to make notes on.

2.   Essential information.

Note the speaker's name and the subject and date so that you can find your notes easily when you want to refer to them afterwards — if, for example, you need to use them for an essay or to prepare an argument. You may want to file them in a different system at a later date. Or you may drop your file and scatter everything! Without headings, sorting them out can be very difficult.

3. Deciding what to write down.

Listen hard — particularly at the beginning. Good lecturers/speakers will outline what they are about to cover and so you'll be able to work out what the important themes are. Often they will write up key headings on a blackboard. Sometimes they will make a point, then spend some minutes giving examples to help you understand. Speakers often repeat themselves. This all helps you.

Most important: *don't attempt to write down everything as the speaker talks*. You'll simply lose the thread and have masses of unconnected detail at the end, if you do. *Jot down the main ideas and important supporting details only*. Use abbreviations and key words and short phrases (never full sentences) to remind you afterwards what it was all about.

In time you will discover how much detail you need to take down to jog your memory when you are rewriting your notes afterwards. You'll discover that it varies. When a subject is familiar you will need far fewer notes than you would for a new topic.

Most people need to write down *dates and numbers* (such as percentages) *and people's names* — it's almost impossible to carry these in our heads. Your system of abbreviations may take quite a while to become easy to use, but persevere — it will help tremendously.

"Don't attempt to write everything down as the speaker talks."

4. Writing it up.

Now the real task begins, after the speaker/ lecturer or discussion has finished. As soon as possible afterwards (certainly the same day), use your jotted notes to stimulate your memory of the talk, and reconstruct the lecture from your jottings into a good set of notes using any of the layouts mentioned in *'Notetaking from Books'* (Chapter 5) — Summary Notes, Outline Notes or Pattern Notes.

Some people find they can actually take down their jottings in a lecture in Outline or Pattern forms, but for most of us it's easier to jot down ideas without having to concentrate on the best way to arrange them. In any case it's the *thinking* that is required when you come to rearrange your jottings which helps your understanding. So it isn't really an advantage to take 'perfect' notes as you listen, because you wouldn't get the chance to think again, remember and reorganise your ideas.

Turning your jottings into Pattern Notes is particularly valuable because you really will have to think hard to decide on the main topic and on the best ways of rearranging key points around the page. Whilst thinking in this way you will often gain new insights into the topic and come to see links between ideas.

You could attempt this stage — the reconstruction of what you heard — without the help of any notes at all. Do this if for any reason you were unable to take notes in the lecture or meeting. But it's best to work from notes: most of us find it very difficult to remember without anything to jog our memories when we come to make a written record.

5. Checking for accuracy.
Unfortunately you can't go back over a lecture or a discussion in the way you can look back over a book to check if your notes are correct. But *you can use other ways of checking*. After you've re-written them go and see the lecturer or speaker if it's possible, to get any uncertainties cleared up. If it's not possible to do this, talk to other people who were listening with you and compare your ideas about what was said.

You could also arrange with fellow students to exchange and compare notes. Checking that your notes are correct, looking at how other people make their notes and exchanging ideas about notetaking, will all improve your ability to make good notes.

6. Filing.
Finally, *decide how to file your notes away*. If you've been reading books and papers on the subject and making notes from these, they can all be grouped together under the appropriate heading. Sometimes you'll want to rewrite one combined set of notes, tying together notes from two or three books and a lecture or discussion, into one full set. That might seem very time-consuming, but the effort of pulling your ideas and notes together into one system will greatly improve your understanding of a subject and, as a result, your ability to remember it.

Finally remember that the thinking and the writing involved in making a clear set of notes will help you to understand whatever you are studying. Even if you were to lose your notes, if you had gone through the process described above you would be able to remember much of what you had written.

Chapter 7

Writing an Essay

Do you tremble at the thought of writing an essay? Do you find you just can't get started? Lots of people do. This chapter gives ideas on organising your thoughts and getting them down, and so makes essay writing a great deal easier and more enjoyable.

A. INTRODUCTION

Lots of us are afraid of essay writing. I hope the advice which follows will help you to feel more confident about it. Don't expect to be able to do all these things straight away: it takes lots of practice (and help from fellow students and your tutor). But with every piece of writing you do you'll get better and better at it. There's an added advantage too. If you get better at essay writing, you'll be better able to write important letters, write work reports, plan talks you may be asked to give etc.

When you are asked to write an essay it's helpful *at first* to follow these stages step by step. But this isn't a list of rules. These are guidelines to help you. They fall into 2 sections. The first (B) deals with planning and preparing for the essay. The second (C) gives some help with actually writing it.

B. PLANNING AND PREPARING

1) Start working on the essay a couple of weeks before it's due in, if you can. Allow yourself plenty of time to think.

2) Read the question *carefully* and consider just what it means and what it's asking you to do. Pay attention to words like 'criticise', 'discuss', 'compare and contrast' and make sure you do just what you are asked. Consult a dictionary if necessary to make sure you fully understand the meaning of the title. One of the worst mistakes made by essay writers is ignoring the title, or changing it to suit themselves.

3) Think up and jot down *questions* which the title suggests to you.

e.g. Title: 'Comment on the decline of industry in Liverpool.'

Possible questions:

a) What industries have there been in the past?

b) Why did they develop?

c) Has there been any decline in these?

d) Why did it happen?

e) Whose fault was it?

f) Have any new industries grown up in place of the lost ones?

   Etc.

4) Check if you already have any notes from lectures, books, films or T.V. programmes etc. which might help you. If you have, gather them all together into a separate folder or file just for this essay. When you have finished it you can put them all back.

5) If you are asked to read certain books or articles for your essay *read purposefully*, trying to find the answers to the questions as you are reading. If you don't read purposefully it'll take far too long and you'll end up with a lot of irrelevant material. Make notes as you read. Make a note of the title, author, publisher and publication date, as well as page references of any books you get your information from. You can then quote titles at the end, and also go back to them later if you need to.

6)   Let your mind wander freely over the subject, *in any direction* and very quickly jot down all your ideas. This is sometimes called 'Brainstorming'. It's amazing how many new ideas can be produced this way. *Better still — do this with a friend*. It's not cheating. You'll both use your ideas differently. Some of the ideas will be discarded later on, but at this point jot down *anything* you think of.

7)   Decide who you are writing this for. It's a good idea to write it to an imaginary friend who is reasonably knowledgeable but doesn't know much about this particular subject, so you'll have to explain what you mean *clearly*. But don't write things you don't believe just to please your reader.

8)   Now take a break for a few days and let the ideas mull around in your head. During this time the subconscious brain gets to work and often comes up with all kinds of ideas at unexpected moments. (Think of how often you've suddenly remembered a name you'd been trying to recall when you're in the bath and no longer thinking about it.) *Trust your brain to work for you — it will*.

If you get a sudden idea during this break, jot it down. It's a good idea to carry a notepad in your bag or pocket, otherwise you may forget again.

"The brain gets to work and often comes up with all kinds of ideas at unexpected moments."

9)   After your break, look back over your jottings and decide which ideas you are going to follow up and which to reject because they don't really answer the question. *The biggest fault most essay writers make is trying to cram every idea in*, with no particular development of theme. You may need to be ruthless now in rejecting ideas and information.

10) Write a brief outline in note form. It's a great help to go back to your own original questions (see note 2 above). The outline should just be paragraph headings with perhaps one or two ideas underneath each heading. *Keep it brief and clear*. In writing your outline you have to decide how you'll present your ideas. There are always several different ways of doing this e.g. if you are asked to examine an argument about a topic, you could:

a) list all the points in favour together, then the points against together, then give your opinions about the topic; or

b) list each point for, then each relevant point against, then your opinion — allowing one paragraph for each point you are considering.

Try out a couple of different ways of laying out your essay in outline form. Then decide which to use and stick to it.

11) Write your first draft, leaving plenty of space between paragraphs so you can add comments later when you re-read it. It's helpful at this stage to write each paragraph under the heading you thought of in your plan.

Put this draft aside for a few days then read it through. Check that your essay is clear, that the argument is well developed etc. *Read it to others, if you can, to get their comments.*

Be prepared to do quite a bit of re-organising of the ideas at this stage to make it clearer.

12) Re-write the essay and check it over.

13) At the end of the essay list the publications you have consulted for information.

C.   SOME POINTS TO REMEMBER WHEN YOU ARE READY TO BEGIN WRITING

1)   It's a good idea to set yourself a time limit for the writing, especially as this is only a first draft.

2)   Before you begin the essay, try to sum up in a few sentences what it's all about. This will help you, as you write each paragraph, to judge whether it's relevant to what you want to say overall.

3)   It's usual to write a short introductory paragraph in which you say what the essay is about and indicate what you will do in the remainder of the essay. It often involves explaining what you understand the title to mean and an explanation of any key words in the title. It gives your reader a sense of direction as she/he goes through your essay.

4)   As you write each paragraph make sure you are answering the question. Sometimes unsure or over-enthusiastic writers wander off the point. Sometimes an essay appears to be a list of unrelated ideas, but if the writer had shown why she/he thought each idea was relevant to the title this could have been avoided. After *each* paragraph ask yourself if it's quite clear how the ideas in it link in to the title.

5)   Don't make sweeping statements. Back each one up by relevant facts, statistics etc. In many essays you are asked to give your opinion, but it's not enough to simply say ''I think x'', you have to *justify* it.

6)   Try to anticipate your reader's criticisms and answer them. If you are writing about 'The Liverpool Riots' and you say: ''The people who took part in the riots were ordinary people who were driven to violence by police harrassment'' the reader is likely to say: ''Is that true? All of them? How do you know that?''. It's better to write: ''Many (or some) of the people who took part in the riots ...'' and *back this up with examples*.

7)   Examples are always useful, but don't fall into the trap of 'padding out' your essay with masses of examples and too few points.

8)   It's a good idea to refer to other people's opinions. But don't just string together a list of opinions. Use them selectively to back your argument, and don't be afraid to be critical of them. Remember to say whose opinion it is and where you found it. If you refer to books and journals, list the titles, dates, authors and chapter, at the end of your essay.

9)   Always be clear — use simple language and reasonably short sentences. Explain all the terms you are using which you may understand, but your reader may not. Don't fall into the trap of assuming that good essays must contain lots of impressive long words and jargon.

10)   Include appropriate illustrations: diagrams, charts, maps etc.

11)   It's not normally necessary either to number your paragraphs or to give them headings in an essay.

12)   The last paragraph usually sums up the main arguments briefly and once again states your view (which has now hopefully been proved!). The final concluding paragraph may closely resemble the summary you wrote before you began (see note 1 above).

13)   Good essay writing is a matter of practice. It's hard at first but soon the points listed above will become second nature to you. To help yourself get better at essay writing it's a good idea to read articles in papers and books. Ask yourself if the writer is doing the sorts of things mentioned above. This will help you to spot 'straight' and 'crooked' thinking in arguments you read and hear in meetings, on the T.V. etc. (For more on this see Chapter 10.)

D. SOME FINAL THOUGHTS

Below is an extract from a book about teaching and learning in Italy. It describes how a group of schoolchildren *collectively* write an essay. *You could try this* with a small group of fellow students, or adapt its approach to working on your own.

"To start with, each of us keeps a notebook in his pocket. Every time an idea comes up, we make a note of it. Each idea on a separate sheet, on one side of the page.

Then one day we gather together all the sheets of paper and spread them on a big table. We look through them, one by one, to get rid of duplications. Next, we make separate piles of sheets that are related, and these will make up the chapters. Every chapter is sub-divided into small piles, and they will become paragraphs.

At this point we try to give a title to each paragraph. If we can't, it means either that the paragraph has no content or that too many things are squeezed into it. Some paragraphs disappear. Some are broken up. While we name the paragraphs we discuss their logical order, until an outline is born. With the outline set, we re-organise all the piles to follow its pattern.

We take the first pile, spread the sheets on the table, and we find the sequence for them. And so we begin to put down a first draft of the text. We duplicate that part so that we each can have a copy in front of us. Then, scissors, paste and coloured pencils. We shuffle it all again. New sheets are added. We duplicate again.

A race begins now for all of us to find any word that can be crossed out, any excess adjectives, repetitions, lies, difficult words, overlong sentences, and any two concepts that are forced into one sentence.

We call in one outsider after another. We prefer it if they have not had too much schooling. We ask them to read aloud. And we watch to see if they have understood what we meant to say.

We accept their suggestions if they clarify the text. We reject any suggestions made in the name of caution.

Having done all this hard work and having followed these rules that anyone can use, we often come across an intellectual idiot who announces, "This letter has a remarkably personal style."

Why don't you admit that you don't know what the art of writing is? It is an art that is the very opposite of laziness."

This extract was taken from a book called *'Letter to a Teacher'* written by the School of Barbiana (Penguin Education).

E. SUMMARY OF THE STEPS YOU CAN TAKE

1) Remember to start the essay well before you need to hand it in.

2) Read the question carefully.

3) Think up questions which the title suggests to you.

4) Check whether you already have any notes on the subject.

5) Read recommended books looking for answers to your questions.

6) Brainstorming — let your mind wander freely round the topic, jot down ideas.

7) Decide who you are writing the essay for.

8) Take a break for a few days and let your brain get to work for you.

9) Look back at your jottings and decide how you'll do the essay.

10) Write a brief outline in note form.

11) Write your first draft. Then take another couple of days break.

12) Go over your draft. Possibly re-organise it. Write your essay. Check it through.

13) List your references.

BOOKS FOR YOU TO READ
1) *How to Study Effectively* by C. Parsons (Arrow) pp. 62-73.
2) *Learn How to Study* by D. Rowntree (Macdonald) pp. 65-78.
3) *How to Study Effectively* by R. Freeman (National Extension College) whole book.
4) *Answer the Question* by C. Moor (National Extension College) whole book.
5) *Writing* by J. Sullivan (National Extension College) whole book.
6) *How to Write Essays* by R. Lewis (National Extension College) whole book (very advanced, but useful).
7) *Writing Essays in the Social Sciences* by T. Sullivan (National Extension College).

Chapter 8

Preparing and Presenting a Talk

Lots of us have to make a speech at different times, to parents' groups at our children's school, to a community or trade union meeting etc. This chapter will be used to look at how to prepare a speech and how to deliver it as well as possible. If you feel nervous of speaking in public this will help you overcome it.

A. INTRODUCTION

Have you ever dreaded having to speak up in front of others, convinced you will forget what you wanted to say, or just that everyone will think you are stupid? Or, more likely, have you remained silent, even though what you wanted to say was important, rather than risk speaking up?

We all have. Even those who appear to be confident. But there are many occasions when we need to speak in public. For example:

when we attend a public meeting and have some point we want to make

or if we agree to play a key part in some group we attend.

There are times when we have to speak to perhaps one or two people, but what we have to say is vitally important and we feel dreadfully anxious in case we don't get it right. For example:

an interview for a job

or meeting our child's teachers to discuss some difficulty

or making a case for better pay

or even just trying to get a fair deal at a shop when returning useless goods.

What all these situations have in common is that what we say and how we say it matters. Because we know that, we usually feel nervous, which makes things worse.

What can we do about it?
As in most other things we can learn about how to do it better, then practise, practise, practise until our confidence to tackle things grows.

On your course of study don't be afraid to take any opportunity you can to speak and especially to give short talks or introduce ideas. *Ask your fellow students and tutors to tell you how you did afterwards.* You need to know your strengths and weaknesses. If you have a chance to see yourself on a video talking to your group, that's a great help too. Perhaps a small group of students could get together to plan a talk on some topic of interest and then each take turns presenting the talk to the rest of the group. Listeners can give helpful advice afterwards. If you feel very nervous, a rehearsal with a friend, or even on your own, can help a lot.

Find whatever ways you can to practise, because developing confidence in your ability to express yourself to others could be the most valuable thing you can learn on any course.

To help you, here are a few useful points to remember as you plan and present a talk. They apply whether you are speaking to an audience or just to one person at an important meeting.

B. PREPARATION

Structuring your speech. In order to present issues clearly *you must be clear about what you want to say.*

1)   To help yourself, make brief notes beforehand about what you want to say, and plan the order of presentation. This is very similar to planning an essay, really.

2)   If there are relevant facts, figures or examples you can give to back up your case, make a note of these.

3)   The structure of the presentation is very important. It should have a) an introduction, b) a body of points and c) a conclusion. This too is similar to an essay.

The introduction should tell people what you intend to say. *You must identify the key points*. If you don't, your listeners may not realise that these are the important points. So if, for example, you start by telling your listeners there are five key points you wish to make they are *prepared* for five points and are less likely to miss them. You can say briefly what the five points are. Then go through each point item by item, backing them up by examples, facts or figures. Then at the end summarise the five points you have given.

It may sound as though you'll be repeating yourself a lot, but in fact it gives a very clear structure to all you are saying and shows your listeners that you have carefully organised your ideas. It helps them to remember them.

When you have prepared your speech don't write it out as you would an essay, or you'll be tempted to keep your eyes down and read it. It's much better to write headings only — with relevant facts or statistics attached. Underline key words in a different coloured pen. *Your sheet of paper needs to be clear*, so that when you glance down at it you can easily find your place. If you can't, you'll be afraid to look up at all.

Better still, *have a set of cards* (postcards will do nicely), *and use a fresh one for each main idea*. Don't cram each card with masses of detail, or you will still have to read it out. Just use a few well-spaced, clearly written words on each. Don't forget to number the cards, or you may get them all mixed, especially if you are nervous.

C. PRESENTATION

1)   Eye contact is important. Look at the people you are talking to, not at your notes or the ceiling. Try to make sure you look at everyone from time to time, not just at the person in front of you.

2)   Don't get side-tracked, or bring in irrelevant details.

3)   Keep it brief. However interested people are, they will begin to lose attention after several minutes.

"However interested people are, they will begin to lose attention after several minutes."

4) Pick out the main points you want to make and emphasise these.

5) Speak clearly, and not too fast. You're very likely to rush if you are nervous.

6) Don't speak in a monotone, or sound as if you are reading. Don't read your speech. Just glance down at the headings on your paper or card, then look up and talk to your audience in a normal conversational tone.

7) Avoid jargon (especially initials) unless you are sure everyone will know what they mean.

8) Use examples to illustrate your points, to help people understand them.

9) Repeat key points to emphasise and reinforce them.

10) Try to avoid distracting, nervous mannerisms, (twiddling your hair, shuffling your feet etc.).

It's often useful to give your listener(s) a brief set of points prepared beforehand on a sheet of paper. This will remind them of what you have said and, maybe, encourage them to act on your suggestions later.

One way of learning how to present information is to watch and listen to others. Notice how they structure their information. What makes one speaker clear and easy to understand and interesting to listen to? What makes another speaker sound muddled, dull etc? Watch people around you, on T.V., listen to them on the radio. You'll pick up a lot of ideas. Then don't be afraid to try them out.

Chapter 9

Graphs and Statistics

So much information in newspapers and textbooks is presented in the form of graphs and statistics and most of us are never taught how to understand them. In this chapter you'll be shown how to read graphs and make sense of statistics.

A. INTRODUCTION

Many adults are afraid of maths. Often, having been badly taught at school, we think we can't understand maths, and when we see graphs or statistics in newspapers we quickly pass them over. Yet so much information nowadays is presented in the form of graphs and statistics (in newspapers and on T.V.) that we all need to understand them and feel confident about reading and interpreting them. We also need to know how statistics and graphs can be used to *lie and deceive*. An excellent and very readable book on this is "*How to Lie with Statistics*" by Darrell Huff (Pelican).

This chapter is meant to serve as an introduction to these subjects. It will show you the different kinds of graphs you may see in newspapers, books, your course notes etc.

"So much information nowadays is presented in the form of graphs and statistics."

B. GRAPHS

There are many different ways of presenting information through pictures rather than through words. That is all graphs are: information in pictures. They *can* be much easier to understand than words.

You will be familiar with most kinds of graph, though you may never have tried to look at them carefully, or read them.

1. Picture Graphs

These are usually very easy to read and understand.

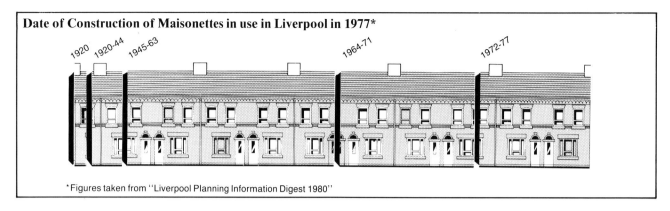

Date of Construction of Maisonettes in use in Liverpool in 1977*

*Figures taken from "Liverpool Planning Information Digest 1980"

> ★ *Try writing out in full sentences all the information you can gather from this graph — and the ones which follow. You'll soon see how much clearer a graph can be than words.* ★

2. Pie Graphs

So called because they are the shape of a pie, each slice representing a proportion of the whole.

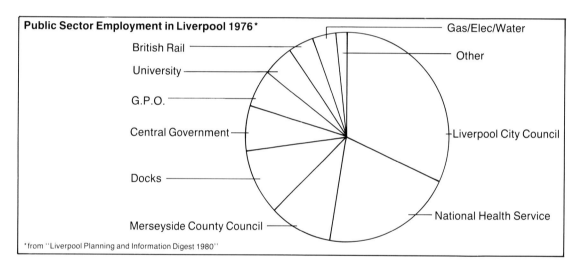

Public Sector Employment in Liverpool 1976*

Gas/Elec/Water
British Rail
Other
University
G.P.O.
Central Government
Liverpool City Council
Docks
National Health Service
Merseyside County Council

*from "Liverpool Planning and Information Digest 1980"

3. Ideo Graphs

Here a symbol is used to represent quantity. Often symbols of the same size are used to represent equal numbers of items.

Expenditure on Services*

*These figures are *not* official statistics

£500 million (Education)
£250 million (Housing)
£200 million (Roads)
£175 million (Law & Order)
£150 million (Health)

4. Histograms (or bar graphs)

These are perhaps the easiest diagrams to construct and read. If each bar is the same width, then all that needs to be looked at is the height difference between the bars.

Male/Female Employment in Liverpool 1971-76

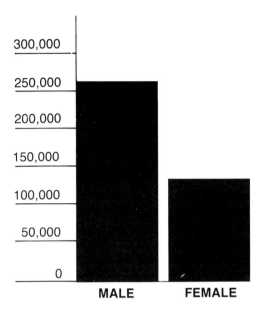

Or the same information can be conveyed in one bar (but this is usually harder to read at a glance).

5. Line Graphs

These are often used to show how something changes over time. You must look carefully at the figures on the left of the graph and those below it, in order to understand the graph.

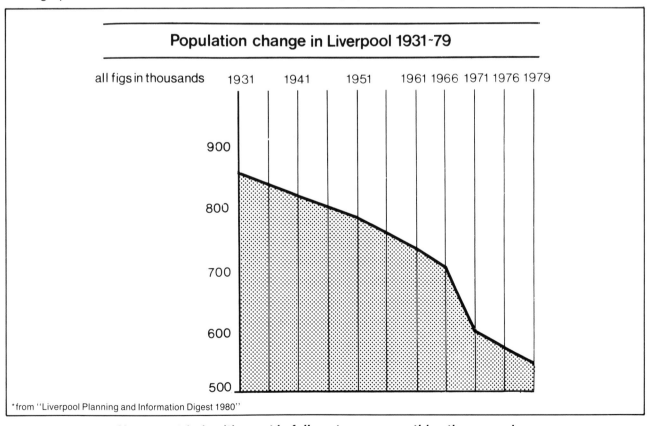

Population change in Liverpool 1931-79

all figs in thousands   1931   1941   1951   1961 1966 1971 1976 1979

* from "Liverpool Planning and Information Digest 1980"

★ *Have you tried writing out in full sentences everything these graphs can tell you? If not, do it now.* ★

Finally here is an example of the same piece of information represented in a variety of ways. It is not based on factual information, so don't quote it!

Animal owners in Broadville — 1982
10,000 families owned a dog
 8,000 families owned a cat
 3,000 families owned a budgie
 1,000 families owned a goldfish

Pie Graph

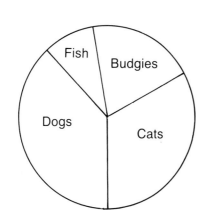

Histogram

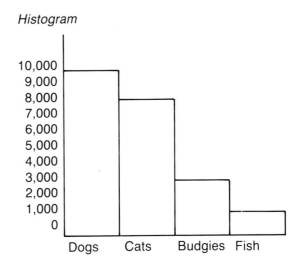

Ideograph

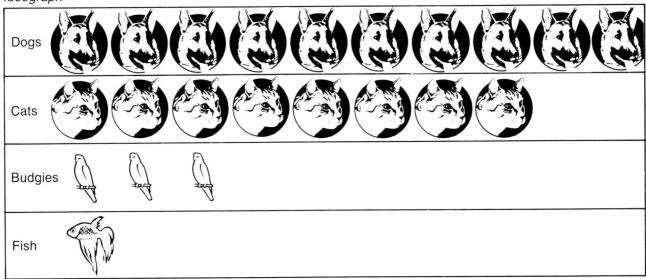

C. STATISTICS

Statistics are everywhere around us.

1. Percentages.

X% now unemployed   Y% read a certain newspaper   Z% own a certain car.

Percentage simply means *per hundred*. So if 85% of households own a fridge that means 85 out of every 100 do. Simple enough.

So how can such clear, simple numbers be used to deceive us? In many ways. Let's look at an example from opinion polls conducted around election time.

First let's look at what percentage of British voters voted for the different political parties in 1983:

Conservative — 42.4%

Labour — 27.6%

SDP/Liberal Alliance — 25.4%

Others — 3.4%

How do we know? *Every vote was counted*.

So why are the *pre-election* surveys conducted by newspapers and other groups so very unreliable? *Because they don't ask everyone in the country*. It would take far too long and cost too much money and lots of people would refuse. So instead they ask a *sample* and they multiply up their results.

Let's say 35 million people can vote in an election. If the opinion poll sample is 100 people, can we rely on its results to predict how the 35 million will vote? Obviously not. If we use even 1,000 it's a very small sample.

So whenever you read the result of a poll the first question to ask is:

"*How many people were asked and what proportion are they of the number of people the poll is supposed to be predicting about?*"

There are many other important questions too. If our poll sample was 1,000 who were they, where did they live, etc? If they all read the 'Telegraph' newspaper then they'll be more likely to vote Conservative. If they all live in the same area, or if they are all women, or if they are of similar ages (and so on) this will making the findings less likely to represent the nation's voting intentions accurately.

So your second question has to be:

"*Who were the people who were asked these questions? How were they selected?*"

Much of the information drawn from surveys and presented to us as fact is incorrect because the sample was *biased* (whether intentionally or not). *A biased sample is one which doesn't really represent the population it's supposed to represent*.

These two points a) the size of a sample and b) how it was selected, are just the first major reasons why so much statistical information is not reliable. There are many other reasons why it might not be. For example:

"*How can we be sure everyone who replied told the truth?*"

Let's suppose that the information gathered from a survey *is* correct, that it doesn't actually lie, how else might we be deceived? Again there are many ways in which information is presented in such a way as to mislead us, and cause us to misinterpret it.

2. Averages.
Suppose five employees of a company earn the following wages:

A — £50,000 — Senior Manager

B — £20,000 — Area Head

C — £10,000 — Supervisor

D — £ 5,000

               Machine Operators

E — £ 5,000

We can quite truthfully be told that the average wage is £18,000 (£90,000 shared by 5).

But what does that mean? When we think of averages we tend to think of it as something *typical* of most people. But £18,000 isn't the wage of any one of the employees.

3. Interpretation.

Figures don't mean anything in themselves. *It's how we interpret them that counts*. And the same set of figures can be interpreted in numerous ways.

Here is an example:

"Recent research has conclusively proved that storks do bring babies. In Germany in the early 20th Century the average family size was 7 children per household. All family homes had numerous chimney stacks at the time, on which storks frequently nested. By the late 1970's the birth rate had dropped dramatically to an average 2 children per household. Few German houses in the 1970's carry the traditional tall chimney stacks and the absence of roosting storks is noticeable. The decline in the stork population has undoubtedly led to the decline in the human population".

★ Can you work out an alternative reason? ★

Could it be that modern centrally heated homes no longer need the old chimney stacks, and that along with modernisation of heating methods has come, quite coincidentally, the modernisation of birth control?

In other words simply because two factors occur together (fewer chimney stacks and lower birth rates) you can't prove one *causes* the other. Both can be caused by a third factor — in this case the developments of science in heating and medicine.

The moral of the story: don't accept proof that one thing causes another — there may be a third factor causing both. How facts are *interpreted* is more important than the facts themselves.

4. Missing Information

Another example shows clearly how statistics can be interpreted falsely.

"More accidents occur in clear weather than they do in conditions of snow and ice."

This is true. But it leads us to think that it's *safer* to drive in snow and ice than on a clear road in good weather.

How does it do that? Because it doesn't point out that there are far more clear days in a year than days of snow and ice. In fact the *proportion* of accidents goes up when weather conditions are bad, as we all know, but the *total number* is still greater on clear days.

What about this for missing information:

"X kills 90% of all known germs."

What about the unknown ones?

This very brief introduction to the deceptions that abound in statistics will alert you to some of them. Read *"How to lie with Statistics"* by Darrell Huff (Penguin) for more. Try spotting them for yourself. Advertisers, politicians etc. use them frequently. Beware of anyone using facts and figures to persuade you to believe things.

Chapter 10

Straight and Crooked Thinking

How often have you listened to someone or read something and thought "I know that's not right but I can't put my finger on what's wrong with it" and so haven't been able to argue back? This chapter explains some of the hundreds of ways speakers and writers attempt to mislead and persuade us by 'crooked thinking'. You'll get lots of chance to practise afterwards — just look in any newspaper!

A. INTRODUCTION

Our ability to think clearly and read and listen critically is clouded by many devices. Some are used intentionally to deceive us, some are not. Whether they are deliberate or not, the end product is nevertheless misleading. Sometimes we are aware that we are being misled, but somehow cannot quite work out what's wrong because the argument we read or hear seems logical. Sometimes we are quite unaware that we are being misled, and happily accept someone's arguments, although they are based on false information. We are especially likely to do this if the person's arguments fit in with our own prejudices.

In this chapter we will examine some of the devices which mislead us, using examples wherever possible. After that it's up to you to be constantly on the lookout for examples of crooked thinking — whether they are deliberate or not. You will find plenty of them in everything you read and hear. Look carefully in newspapers (especially the 'letters' pages) and the books you read. Listen to speakers on T.V. news and current affairs programmes etc.

As you develop the ability to see through crooked thinking you will be better able to *read critically* and to *think clearly*. You should also become better at writing clearly, because you will be far more aware of the pitfalls of vagueness, or of not backing up a case with relevant proof.

B. CROOKED ARGUMENT

Here are some of the devices which, whether used deliberately or not, mislead us.

1. Using persuader words and phrases.
Words which make you feel you must agree:

e.g. *'obviously'*, *'clearly'*, *'surely'* etc.

Once you read one of these words or phrases you may forget to look carefully at the argument:

"As everyone knows this government has done more to help the sick and needy than any other."

It may be true. It may not. But where is the *proof* for this sweeping statement?

2. Emotive language.
This means trying to influence people by using words which appeal to their feelings. This technique is used a great deal in advertising:

e.g. *"Kellogg's Cornflakes — The Sunshine Breakfast"*.

Sunshine is such a happy, pleasant thought for most of us that we are more likely to buy the product, especially when appealing pictures are added.

This language is used in politics particulary, and a great deal in the press.

e.g. *"These mindless thugs have the economy by the throat."*

'Thug' is used to conjure up images of people whose aim is to destroy our society — and the image of *'have our economy by the throat'* conjures up a strong, brutal, murderous aggressor attacking its helpless victim.

This is powerful language which seriously affects our ability to think clearly and read critically. The best way to deal with it is to replace all *emotive* words with *neutral* ones.

Try it with "*These thugs have the economy by the throat*". If you rewrite it as "*These trade unionists are putting the economy under considerable pressure*" — it sounds *very* different.

★ **Look through today's paper. Find any emotive words, underline them, and try to replace them with neutral words.** ★

There are times however when using emotive language is perfectly appropriate — in poetry and other creative writing for example; and of course it can liven up conversation and writing generally. It may also be fairly used when we wish to spur people into taking action. *But beware of emotive language in newspapers, politics, the law, religion, and anywhere where it is being used to influence opinions and decisions.*

"Emotive language can be fairly used when we wish to spur people into taking action."

3. Analogy and metaphor.
Two more devices very closely linked with the emotive language device are analogy and metaphor.

a) Analogy

"*This Company is like one big happy family: we all work together for the good of all*."

In analogy we say one thing *is like* another, and it can be very helpful because it may link an unfamiliar idea to a familiar one and so help us understand the unfamiliar one. The trouble comes when we move on to *draw conclusions* which don't necessarily follow:

"*The Director of the Company will do nothing which will harm any worker's interests*".

This is obviously not true. They may make workers redundant and when they do, those workers will no longer be "members of the family". Although it may help the Company (even the remaining workers), it certainly won't help the individual workers who became redundant.

Let us look at another example:

"*The family is like a tree: the parents are like the roots, the children are like the branches.*"

This is a reasonable analogy explaining fairly clearly how closely linked the members of a family are. But if we push the analogy further and argue:

"*... so to separate a child from its natural parents is akin to murder: the branches cannot survive without their roots.*"

Here we are using a *false analogy* because the similarity between trees and families isn't all that great. There are many differences, and we know that children can and do survive without their natural parents. Yet arguments like this are frequently heard in courts as lawyers argue over the custodial rights of parents versus foster parents. They are deliberately trying to cloud the judgement of the jurors by using analogy.

b) Metaphor
This is very similar to analogy and can be used in the same way to cloud our judgement. Like analogy, metaphor can be very useful when we are trying to understand something unfamiliar. But, like analogy, metaphor is usually misused when it is used to try to persuade us. In metaphor we say *something is something else*, whilst in analogy we say it is *like* something else.

e.g. To talk about "*The Ship of State needs a firm hand at the helm*"

is to use a metaphor. The metaphor here is to say the State *is* a ship.

> ★ **Think about this one. List any ways in which you think the State is like a ship, and then list the ways in which the State isn't like a ship.** ★

This is a good technique for dealing with any metaphors and analogies, and using it soon helps you spot false conclusions and enables you to argue back.

4. Generalisation.
This means making a statement about all or most of a group which is based on only a few instances:

e.g. "*All politicians are power hungry*"

or "*The police force today is bent*".

Some politicians are 'power hungry' and some policemen are 'bent' — but we must be very careful of generalisations like this unless concrete proof is offered.

Of course some generalisations are useful and generally true:

e.g. "*It will be cold in Alaska in winter. Take plenty of warm clothing when you go*".

But generalisations should always be treated with great caution when used to influence our opinions or actions, and when any subject is controversial. Be careful of making generalisations in your writing too. Check if they are reasonable. Do they need evidence to support them?

To deal with a generalisation you should ask the speaker for *evidence* — for proof that the statement applies to all cases. It's then easy to spot just how you have been misled.

5. Making appeals.
Another set of devices is to appeal to a) authority b) tradition c) force and d) pity in order to persuade others.

a) Appeal to authority
e.g. "*I know it's true. I read it only last week in the Guardian*".

or "*As Professor A says, the world's climate is changing and we are entering a second ice age.*"

If Professor A is a geographer or a climatologist then his or her opinion may well be worth listening to, and that may be a fair use of appeal to authority. If, however, Professor A is a professor of French, there is no reason whatsoever to accept an opinion merely because she/he holds it.

So if you hear or read an argument which is simply an appeal to authority, don't accept it. Demand proof.

b) Appeal to tradition
e.g. *"We've always done it this way"*

or *"If it was good enough for your father and me, then it's good enough for you."*

These examples show that this is simply an *appeal*, not an argument because in fact *the opposite* can be used with just as much force.

e.g. *"New formula X gets washing whiter."*

Here the suggestion is that the powder must be better simply because it's a *new* formula. Neither the appeal to tradition nor the appeal to novelty (newness) is *proof* of anything — so don't be misled by them. Look for proof.

c) Appeal to force
Threats and blackmail are good examples of this. The sole reason for doing something is fear of the consequences rather than belief that it's the best thing to do. But the appeal to force can be far more subtle than that. When a campaigner uses a petition signed by hundreds to persuade Parliament to do something, the campaigner is saying:

"It must be right to do X when so many people support it".

But sheer force of numbers doesn't automatically make something right. The majority of the British population probably supports the return of hanging. Does that make it *right*?

d) Appeal to pity
This is often used in courts etc.:

The defence asks the jury not to find A guilty of theft because to send him to gaol would break up his family.

Whatever the *consequences* of punishing A might be, it has nothing to do with determining whether or not he *committed the crime* in question.

All these appeals are used a great deal in all advertising
> ★ **Look through adverts in the papers and on T.V. and try to spot some of the appeals.** ★

They are also used a lot by politicians. So whenever you think the speaker/writer is *appealing* to you to believe something or take some action, *take care*. Make sure a good case has been made out already and *don't be persuaded by the appeal **alone***.

6.   False cause.
This means suggesting that one thing *causes* another because one occurred *before* the other:

e.g. *In some societies when the sun was eclipsed, the religious leaders would offer a human sacrifice to the Gods and the sun would soon reappear.*

They believed the sacrifice appeased the Gods who then allowed the sun to return. This was *clear proof to them* that the Gods took away the sun: human sacrifice appeased their anger and so they reversed their action. We now know this to be an inaccurate explanation of an eclipse of the sun. But we still continually make the mistake of linking two events together and saying one causes the other when there is no *proof* of causality. This can be used deliberately as a device to mislead us.

False cause is often very hard to spot. But we must be constantly on our guard to detect it. Once again the way to deal with it is to ask the speaker (or examine the author's writing) for proof that one thing causes another. (See page 44 for an example of false cause).

7.   Rhetorical questions.
Compare these two questions. In what way are they different?
Question 1: *"Are you hungry yet?"*

Question 2: *"Isn't it time you lot stopped moaning and got back down to work?"*

Question 2 isn't a real question because there is only one possible answer. It's a rhetorical question. *It's really an emotive statement*. It's a bit like the 'persuader words'. It puts pressure on us to agree, and it deceives us because we often think we have reached that conclusion *ourselves*, because we've answered the question. In fact it wasn't a question at all.

8. Irrelevance.
Another device is to try to lead us away from one point by introducing another:

e.g. *"It's a waste of time trying to get rid of nuclear weapons until we've done something about road accidents because more people died from road accidents than from nuclear war last year."*

It may be true that they have, but this isn't an argument for abandoning the principle of abolishing nuclear weapons. Why not attempt to do something about both weapons and road accidents?

It's a form of argument used a lot by politicians to persuade electors against taking expensive steps to correct something. Even if X is worse than Y it doesn't prove you should ignore Y.

9. The average.
A very commonly used misleading device is to say that our own view lies between two extremes and so must be the best. We are all inclined to slip into this way of arguing, especially politically, where many of us tend to see ourselves as moderately placed between other extremists. Remember that just because someone can prove that their view lies halfway between two extremes doesn't in any way prove that it's the best. It's simply *appealing to our desire to compromise*.

The rise in the popularity of the SDP Party is a good recent example of the political use of appealing to the midway point between two extremes. The fact that SDP policies lie somewhere between Tory and Labour views doesn't prove that they are the best policies for the nation. They could be, but not just because they lie between the others.

10. Slandering the opponent.
By *abusing the personality of the speaker* we try to disprove the truth of her/his statements. This is a device very commonly used in politics — and in particular at election times — when, instead of examining policies, the parties indulge in 'mud slinging'. The press campaigns against Tony Benn or to a lesser extent against Norman Tebbitt are good examples of this: discrediting the man in order to discredit his policies, instead of examining the policies. All political parties resort to this device regularly. Read any paper for proof of this.

11. Vested interest.
In accusing someone of *self interest* we imply that she/he must be lying because she/he has something to gain or lose personally:

e.g. *If a wealthy man argues against increases in Income Tax we may reject his arguments because he has much to gain by persuading us to agree.*

However that does not mean his arguments are wrong, and we should listen just as carefully to them as we would if he had no personal involvement. As we listen we should remember that he has much to gain, but not dismiss his ideas because of it.

C. SOME DISHONEST TRICKS

Now let us look at some of the things which can occur when two or more people are engaged in an argument about their opinions and beliefs. Here is a list of some of the dishonest tricks used deliberately to defeat an opponent's argument unfairly.

1) Driving your opponent into exaggerating his original claims and so making unsupportable statements:

e.g. *In discussing Russia and the Eastern Bloc countries, A may begin by saying that in some respects citizens of these countries are better off than some in western capitalist countries. B may goad A into stating that everything is marvellous in communist countries. B can then use any one incident to disprove this last statement and so B can appear to have won the argument.*

2) Extending your opponent's argument:

e.g. *A, a pacifist, argues he won't kill an enemy in defence of his country.*

B says that A then shouldn't kill a madman threatening his children's lives.

That's an unfair trick. There is no reason why B should extend A's argument to a totally different set of circumstances. If B gets A to say he would defend his children from a madman, it doesn't mean A should kill an enemy in war. *They are different circumstances.*

3)   "*It's the exception that proves the rule.*"
Don't be fooled. Exceptions do not prove rules. This is an old fashioned use of the word prove. 'Prove' used to mean 'test'. So that saying really means "*It's the exception that **tests** the rule*".

4)   Diversion.
e.g. "*A says he disapproves of apartheid because black South Africans are oppressed politically.*

B says black people in South Africa are financially better off than anywhere else in Africa."
B's statement *may* be true, but it's *irrelevant* because it has nothing to do with whether or not black people are oppressed *politically* and that was the original statement.

5)   Fastening on a trivial and incorrect part of an argument, proving it's untrue and thereby 'proving' all the argument is untrue.

6)   Putting forward an extreme case to start with, then as the argument progresses, substituting a more moderate statement. When the more moderate statement is accepted, then the speaker *appears* to have won the argument. This is similar to taking up a negotiating position in wage bargaining. It may be quite justifiable in wage bargaining, but it's not justifiable when you are seeking to find the truth of an argument.

All of these tricks can be foiled by insisting on going back to your own or your opponent's *original statement* at all times. It's a good idea to write down your opponent's and your own original statements as they can easily get lost in an argument.

D.   PREJUDICES AND HABITS OF THOUGHT

Finally let us look at how our *Prejudices* and *Habits of Thought* can cloud our own judgement and cause us to deceive *ourselves* and others. This chapter has been written in such a way as to alert us to the devices which others may use to mislead us. But it's important to be aware that *we all use these forms of crooked thinking ourselves* and we must be constantly watching out for them in our *own* speech and writing as well as in that of others.

1.   Prejudices.
We all have prejudices. Very often we are unaware of them because we are so convinced we are correct that we don't see them as prejudices but simply as facts. So we use all our powers of reasoning to back up our prejudices. And we are particularly likely to accept without question the opinions of others who share our prejudices. We are not being hypocritical, but we are deceiving ourselves.

How can we avoid this?

First, by examining closely any beliefs we have which serve our own interest:

e.g. *If I am rich, do I support Tories because they will allow me to keep more of what I can make?*

or *If I am poor, do I believe in socialism because I will get a bigger share of the cake myself?*

It doesn't follow that that *is* my reason for supporting one party or the other, but I should certainly question it.

Second, we should pay close attention to any arguments put *against* something we believe in:

e.g. *If I am a passionate supporter of CND, it's even more important that I should listen carefully to all the arguments for continuing to maintain nuclear weapons.*

Darwen, when constructing his Theory of Evolution, kept a notebook of every opposing fact or opinion he heard, because he wisely realised *we tend to forget anything we don't agree with and exaggerate what we do agree with.*

If we pay attention to the views which contradict our own it can help us in another way. If we finally decide that our own views are correct, we are *much* better able to argue convincingly against those who hold opposing views.

2. Habits of thought.

These are just as misleading as prejudices. They are not quite the same thing though.

e.g. *We don't rethink our ideas on socialism or capitalism every time we vote.*

But this in itself can lead us to be duped. We must be prepared to rethink our ideas from time to time.

We have all developed certain habits of thought simply *because of how, where and when we are brought up*, and all our judgements are made according to our experiences and the habits of thought they develop in us. By studying and understanding other cultures and other historical periods we can begin to understand the limitations of our own habits of thought and begin to understand other people's thoughts.

It's because we can't enter properly into others' habits of thought that most quarrels begin. This applies as much to quarrels between nations (wars) as it does to quarrels between individuals.

It's important for us to recognise that the beliefs we accept *can* be questioned, to recognise how they were formed and to be ready to question them at all times; just as it's important to be ever watchful for the many devices which may cloud our thinking.

The many examples you have studied in these pages are only the tip of the iceberg. We deceive one another (and ourselves) in many ways. Getting good at spotting them and being able to argue back effectively is something that grows with practice. You will never be short of examples to practice on. They occur everywhere, from conversations in pubs, to political line ups on T.V. question programmes. They are everywhere in newspapers and books. Start looking now, and don't ever stop.

BOOKS FOR YOU TO READ

This chapter can only serve as an introduction to what is a rather complex subject. There are several very good books and chapters of books which you may wish to go on to read. They include:

1) *Straight & Crooked Thinking* by R. H. Thouless (Pan).
2) *Reading and Understanding* by T. Sullivan (National Extension College) Chapters 3 and 4.
3) *Clear Thinking* by Inglis and Lewis (National Extension College) Chapters 4 and 5.
4) *Learning To Study* by G. Gibbs (National Extension College) Chapters 3 and 4.
5) *Mastering Study Skills* by R. Freeman (Macmillan Master Series) Chapter 6.

Bibliography

Below is a list of some of the books especially written to help mature students learn how to study. Many of them are workbooks with plenty of practical exercises to try out. Don't rush out and buy them. Borrow some from your tutors or your local library (they'll order you copies if they don't stock them). Try them out and then if you want to buy any you'll know which are most suitable for you.

	Title	Author	Publisher
1.	*Learn How To Study*	D. Rowntree	Macdonald
2.	*How To Study Effectively*	C. Parsons	Arrow
3.	*How To Study Effectively*	R. Freeman	National Extension College
4.	*Mastering Study Skills*	R. Freeman	Macmillan Master Series
			National Extension College
5.	*Learning To Study*	G. Gibbs	National Extension College
6.	*Studying*	T. Sullivan	National Extension College
7.	*Writing*	T. Sullivan	National Extension College
8.	*How To Write Essays*	R. Lewis	National Extension College
9.	*Writing Essays In Social Sciences*	T. Sullivan	National Extension College
10.	*Reading and Understanding*	T. Sullivan	National Extension College
11.	*Clear Thinking*	J. Inglis & R. Lewis	National Extension College
12.	*Answer the Question*	C. Moor	National Extension College
13.	*How to Use Your Dictionary*	R. Lewis & M. Pugmire	Pelican
14.	*Read Better: Read Faster*	M. & E. De Leeuw	David & Charles
15.	*Speed Reading*	T. Buzan	David & Charles
16.	*Speed Memory*	T. Buzan	Pan
17.	*Straight and Crooked Thinking*	R. H. Thouless	Penguin
18.	*How to Lie With Statistics*	Darrell Huff	B.B.C. Publications
19.	*Use Your Head*	T. Buzan